DEDICATION

To the memory of my parents, Lilo and Erwin Camp.

To my wife, Melanie, and our daughters, Elizabeth and Stephanie, for their love, support and assistance.

ALSO BY STEVEN C. CAMP

MONEY: 127 Answers
To Your Most-Asked Financial Questions

and

MONEY Matters Made Easy

Contents

Acknowledgments **7**

Introduction **9**

Chapter 1   **Evaluating Investments** 11
   Interview with Richard Marston .. 25
   Interview with Jeremy Siegel 47

Chapter 2   **Economic Influences** 59
   Interview with Harry Dent, Jr. 75

Chapter 3   **Understanding Stocks and Bonds** . 99
   Interview with Lloyd Kurtz 119
   Interview with Andrew Barrett 146

Chapter 4   **Planning for Retirement** 161
   Interview with Dr. Gigi Hirsch 175

Chapter 5   **All About IRA's** 191

Chapter 6   **Reducing Taxes** 211

Chapter 7   **Paying for College** 219

Chapter 8   **Understanding Estate Planning** ... 231

Chapter 9   **Insurance / Home Ownership** 243

Chapter 10   **Personal and Family Matters** 259
   Interview with CEO and
   CFO Medsite.com 274

Index   (Chapter-Question No.) 281

Acknowledgments

The most gratifying aspect of writing a personal financial column or book is when I learn how readers have improved their lives as a result of reading and following my advice. I thank Greg Kelly and Randy Robbin of *Physician's MONEY DIGEST* for providing me a forum to try to answer physician's questions and address their financial concerns.

I wish to acknowledge Ellen Guest for her editing support, Betsy Lampé for designing the book cover and Betty Wright for transforming a manuscript into book form.

Special thanks for checking the accuracy of the contents to Dr. Roscoe Brady Humberto Cruz, Fred Goldsmith, Steve Gordon, Jeff Kahn, Susan Kerr, Anita Kotler, Dr. Jon Kotler, Ralph Leach, Dr. Dennis Maki, Kathleen Murray, Tom Northcutt, Steve Peltz, Dr. Barbara Rommer, Jim Russell, Sandy Schmidt, Jay Shein, Jean Sorenson, Randy Stockton.

Introduction

Since October 1998, I've had the privilege of fielding a wide array of financial questions from physicians nationwide in my "Answerman" column of *Physician's MONEY DIGEST*. This column is read by 150,000 physicians nationwide, and is published 19 times a year by Medical World Business Press of Jamesburg, New Jersey.

In October 1999, *Physician's MONEY DIGEST* invited me to go one step further by sharing with its readers a series of interviews I've conducted with some of the best experts in the financial world today. We called it "the PMD Answerman gets to ask the questions." I feel privileged to share these interviews with you.

We started with well-known futurist and demographer, Harry Dent, who gave us a crystal clear look into his economic crystal ball. Then, a few months later while I was reading my college alumni magazine, the "Pennsylvania Gazette," I was delighted to discover an article about four recent alumni from the PENN Class of '93. They'd recently started an Internet company called Medsite.com, an online home to help physicians make their practices survive and thrive in today's current turbulent and changing medical world. I'd graduated about 30 years earlier than these four motivated entrepreneurs, but was most intrigued to hear their stories.

Being associated with a major Wall Street organization, I'm fascinated by some of the brilliant people I've been privileged to be in contact with. One is Andrew Barrett, the technology guru, and another is Lloyd Kurtz, the healthcare guru. Besides being genuinely modest, Andrew and Lloyd have a knack for discussing technical and complicated subjects in a way that you and I can understand them.

As an alumnus of the Wharton School, I'm especially

proud to have interviewed two distinguished faculty members — Professors Jeremy Siegel and Richard Marston. In their interviews, they graciously shared their opinions about the current and future state of the economy and stock market, about investing for retirement, and about preparing a child for college and a successful career.

Last year, while I was driving home and listening to "Marketplace" on National Public Radio, David Brancaccio was interviewing Dr. Gigi Hirsch. I heard her say, "Physicians currently represent a profession in crisis." And, as you can imagine, it captured my attention. I knew our readers would be as interested as I was in hearing from her. Dr. Hirsch, a psychiatrist, and formerly an instructor at the Harvard Medical School, founded MDIntelliNet, a healthcare placement and consulting firm for physicians. In our interview that you'll find inside, she talks about how she coaches and counsels physicians disillusioned with their career choice because of financial and non-financial pressures.

The interviews with the experts I've mentioned above appeared in abridged form in *Physician's MONEY DIGEST* because of space limitations. This book contains the complete interview plus 207 questions from readers with my answers.

Steven C. Camp

Chapter 1
Evaluating Investments

Many of the inquiries I receive from physicians deal with evaluating individual investments to structure investment portfolios. Frequently, they will amass collections of sundry securities without having an overall plan. The result may be portfolios with components that prevent them from achieving their personal financial goals. These portfolios may lack diversification and be collections of equities from two or three sectors such as health care, technology or the Internet. These types of portfolios may expose these physicians to much greater risks than they can comfortably handle.

Because each of us is unique and has a different financial objective, risk tolerance, investment experience, time frame and amount of money to commit; we need to structure portfolios with which we are comfortable. With so many investment options and conflicting opinions, what should an investor do?

By managing risk through asset allocation and diversification while maintaining a long-term perspective, your investment journey will be less bumpy and stressful. As your personal situation changes, you may wish to gradually modify your investment objectives.

Following this chapter are individual interviews with two leading Wharton finance professors, Richard Marston and Jeremy Siegel, as they share their opinions on economic influences and on evaluating investments.

1

As a single 30-year-old first time investor/doctor with no debts, I have the following questions:

a. Never having invested in the stock market, do you think it is wise to enter it when everyone seems to be saying that the market is overvalued? What I fear is losing more capital before a serious market correction. What I fear even more is losing more money by not being in the market.

If you are concerned about losing your money because of a major downturn in the markets, don't invest all of it at once. Instead use dollar cost averaging on a weekly or monthly interval, regardless of market conditions add to your investment account on schedule. When the markets go down, you get a bonus buying more shares at cheaper prices.

You are correct in writing that you face a greater threat of not being in the market for the long term because your money market funds will stagnate because of inflation and taxes. Since 1995, many well-known pundits have said today's stock market is overvalued. Let's examine the Dow 30 Average over the past five years as of the last business day in July. If we had listened to the warnings, refused to invest in the market because of its high prices and remained in cash, we would have felt exasperated.

1995 4,708   1996 5,528   1997 8,222
1998 8,883   1999 10,655

b. Do you recommend that I take more risks than usual since I'm only 30? Is this prudent?

For funds invested for retirement, you will not be touching this money earlier than 2027. Between then and now, you can ride the ups-and-downs of the equity markets. Be well-diversified in growth investments, use asset allocation techniques and you will be well rewarded when you retire. Concentrate on companies with real unit growth not just revenue or profit growth alone especially as we enter deflationary periods when corporate gross margins tend to collapse. For monies you need in less than five years, you may wish to invest in more income producing assets since the equity market cycle may be down when you need to cash out to buy a home or finance a major purchase.

2

Where is the best place to invest my money today to get maximum returns?

Historically, the best place to invest your money is where and when no one else wants to invest theirs — like in emerging markets or severely depressed small cap stocks. Many investors make the mistake of investing in last year's winners. They assume that the upward price momentum won't stop. But this investment strategy almost guarantees that you'll "buy high and sell low." John Templeton, founder of the Templeton mutual fund group and regarded by Wall Street as one of the world's wisest investors, says, "Invest where no one else wants to." That is the best place to invest your money. So if your goal is maximum returns and your investment horizon is long, Templeton's advice makes sense for you.

3

How can I know if I'm investing beyond my risk tolerance or comfort level?

Here's a foolproof test — it works every time. If you wake up in the middle of the night with a burning sensation in your stomach because you're worried about the soundness of your portfolio, then you're investing beyond your comfort level. As physicians, don't you sometimes tell your patients that "your health is more important than your money?" If you're losing sleep over your investments, the stress you'll feel over risky investments during a market correction may not be worth the added returns you'll receive during a bull market.

4

Isn't the S&P 500 the best sector to invest in? During the past five years it has more than doubled. I am 52 and plan to retire when I am 60.

Yes, the S&P 500 has been the best market or sector during the past five years. It has outperformed small stocks, long term bonds, foreign stocks and Treasury bills. But does that always make the S&P 500 the best investment? *No.* Let's examine some returns over the past two decades for five markets and see the benefits of diversification.

1. Foreign stocks (industrial countries)
2. Long term U.S. Government bonds
3. S&P 500 stocks
4. Small Cap domestic stocks
5. Treasury bills

When you look at the best-performing markets since 1980 you'll find that, before 1995, the largest annual returns *did not* come from the S&P 500. The S&P 500 was the best performer in only two of these 14 years. As an investor, you need to diversify your mix of investments by being in asset classes with little correlation. Then, if one asset class or market drops, it doesn't drag down your whole portfolio.

5

I frequently hear the expression "long-term investing." Exactly how long is "long-term"?

"Long term" means something different for different kinds of securities. In general, it means giving an investment the amount of time it needs to bear fruit. Long-term bonds have maturity rates of 10 years or more. And if you're investing in stocks, "long term" is generally five years or more. So if you invest in stocks hoping they'll appreciate in time for your child's college tuition payment in two or three years, you may be disappointed. Especially if there is a temporary market correction and your account value has shrunk just at the exact time you need to write that check.

6

With the market decline I've been spending most of the time watching cable TV financial news because I am worried about my portfolio. It has been an emotional roller coaster and gives me a lot of stress. Any suggestions?

Yes, I suggest you watch less television. If you must watch, switch to ESPN, The Discovery Channel or The Weather Channel. Can you imagine a retiree concerned about her personal health watching medical/health TV programs 6 or 8 hours a day? Almost every show would make that person wonder if she had a new disease. Sound outlandish? Many people have become glued to financial news programs and become emotionally exhausted when the Dow whipsaws 500 plus points in one session.

Until recently, the past 10 years has been one of the most stable periods of rising stock prices. Unfortunately, it lulled many investors into believing that we would never again go through cyclical stock market corrections or see the return of a bear market. Before our current decline, many of these investors wanted aggressive returns and told their advisors or themselves, "I can handle the ups-and-downs of the market and I'm in it for the long haul." All the while, they weren't really prepared for the natural cyclical realities of the market. Some of these aggressive investors were shocked by the most recent general sell-off and forgot they were long term investors. Fearing further losses, they bailed out. Recent redemptions from stock mutual funds were $8 billion. Additions of new capital to these same funds averaged $20 billion monthly.

I suggest that investors step back from the day-to-day market and project themselves two years in the future. When they look back at our current price levels of world class companies, they'll say "What an incredible buying opportunity, why didn't I see it!" I believe our economy is very strong. Inflation is less than two percent, unemployment is less than five percent and interest rates are dropping to new lows. All of these are positive signs for equities. Don't fall into the trap of substituting illogical, irrational exuberance for pessimism.

7

How can I develop a "sell" discipline with equities?

Most recommendations by equity analysts at brokerage firms and banks are on the "buy" or "hold" side, not on the "sell" side. Many investors are completely objective when evaluating whether or not to buy a stock, but the decision to sell is saturated with emotion. Here are seven questions you should ask yourself to become more objective about making "sell" decisions:

1. If you were not already a stockholder, would you buy this stock now? If not, why keep it?
2. Has the stock reached the price objective you set when you bought it?
3. What does the financial professional who sold you this stock advise?
4. Have the fundamentals of the company or the outlook for the industry or economy changed?
5. Are there better potential opportunities elsewhere — with greater rewards and less risk for this money?
6. Has the key management of the company changed? If so, is it better or worse?
7. Are you mistakenly allowing taxes to influence your decision about whether to hold or sell?

8

What is the difference between the earnings yield and price earnings?

Both are ratios that use the same components. Earnings yield= earnings per share divided by market price per share; price earnings = market price per share divided by earnings per share. For example, if the market price of a company is $60 and its earnings per share is $3, the PE (price earnings ratio) is 20 (60/3=20) and the earnings yield is five percent (3/60 = .05 or five percent).

$$\text{Earnings yield} = \frac{\text{Earnings per share}}{\text{Market price}} = \frac{\$3}{\$60} = .05 \text{ or } 5\%$$

$$\text{Price earnings} = \frac{\text{Market price}}{\text{Earnings per share}} = \frac{\$60}{\$3} = 20$$

9

I am a 37-year-old nurse who will not be eligible to join my employer's retirement plan until I have been here for one year. What do you recommend I do in the meanwhile? I have not as yet started to save for retirement and know I am late in getting started.

By recognizing this situation and getting started investing for retirement and just not saving for retirement, you have at least 20-plus years to make up for lost time. Get the names of several competent financial advisors from people you know and trust; and then interview them and narrow your selection to the one you are most comfortable with. When you meet with your prospective advisor, you should be asked lots of questions about your personal financial goals, risk tolerance, if you have a will and durable power of attorney, your current income, assets and debts. If your prospective financial advisor wants to sell you a specific investment without knowing your answers to the above questions, move on to someone else.

If you think you found the right advisor, ask about the benefits of opening a Roth IRA and investing $2,000 in a growth mutual fund with dividends being reinvested. If you are unable to find a competent financial advisor, please let me know and I'll help you find one. Remember, no one cares about your money as much as you do. You need to understand any investments you make and will not invest your money in investments you do not understand nor feel less than 100 percent comfortable with.

Remember that your time horizon is 20 or more years and your investments will fluctuate in value with the ups and downs of the stock market. Don't panic when the market drops a lot and your account value shrinks. You are actually buying more shares at a cheaper price with your reinvested dividends.

Once you have enrolled in your employer's plan, continue funding your Roth IRA with annual contributions of $2,000. If you are looking for growth, make sure you invest in equities in both your retirement plan and Roth IRA — and not in money markets, government investment contracts and corporate bonds or government bonds, which are not considered as growth vehicles.

10

What about these web sites offering callable CDs at better rates than local brokers? How do I check out these places before I send them a lot of money? What do you think about callable CDs as part of a retirement portfolio?

I checked some of the web sites you mentioned. Then I checked with the CD department of a major brokerage firm. Current rates for CDs are: five years — 10 years — 15 years, seven percent — 7.4-7.625 percent — 7.75-8.0 percent. So how can a CD be advertised at 9.25 percent? Especially when the above-market rates are considerably less? Here's the catch: the 9.25 percent rate is usually for only one year and then plunges to seven percent for the remaining 14 years. CD rates would have to drop 200 basis points (two percent) for the CD to be called. The CD holder is stuck with approximately 7.4 percent return for a 15 year CD. I suggest that you deal with a major brokerage firm that values its reputation. And here's another thought. In my opinion, CDs may not make good investments for most retirement portfolios, because they're not flexible and they barely keep up with inflation and taxes.

11

What are alternative investments? Why have I not heard about them before? Who invests in them?

You may not of heard of these investments because the SEC restricts offerings to qualified investors. Qualified investors are institutional investors (institutions with a minimum of $25 million of assets) or high net-worth individuals (with $5 million of investable assets). Normally qualified investors make a minimum commitment of $500,000. Alternative investments have become even more popular recently among qualified investors because of the benefits of portfolio diversification, low correlation with public equity investments and the potential for enhanced risk adjusted returns over the public markets.

Some alternative investments have been characterized as a "pre-IPO offering." Alternative investments are private, non-traditional investment vehicles including private equity funds, venture capital funds, hedge funds, exchange funds, oil and gas funds, real estate opportunity funds and leverage buyout funds. Alternative investments are not mass marketed.

12

What is an exchange fund?

Qualified investors can diversify highly appreciated, low-cost basis stock, tax-free via exchange funds. These exchange funds allow investors with a large holding in one stock to diversify into a basket of securities without having to pay capital gains taxes immediately. This investment strategy appeals to individuals who have a disproportionate share of their net worth in one stock, realize the risk of non-diversification and want to postpone paying the 20 percent capital gains tax.

13

I have some money in my checking account and have been waiting for a dip in the market. Is this it? What do you recommend that I do?

No one knows when the market is at a low or high. Trying to predict market highs or lows is futile. If you are a long-term investor (five or more years), today may be a good time to invest. Where do I think the market will be five years from now? I believe it will probably be up even though past performance is no guarantee for future performance.

14

Should we form a partnership or corporation when starting an investment club among 18 members?

The National Association of Investment Clubs (NAIC) recommends general partnerships because of the cost of forming a corporation. For further information, call NAIC at 810-583-6242 or fax 810-583-4880.

15

Are the CDs my wife and I maintain FDIC insured up to $100,000 per institution?

No. Deposits maintained in different categories of legal ownership are separately insured by the FDIC to $100,000 cap. For example, if you and your wife had joint accounts, individual accounts and IRAs, all would be eligible for the maximum insurance coverage as follows:

Husband	$100,000
Wife	$100,000
Joint	$200,000
Husband's IRA	$100,000
Wife's IRA	$100,000
Total FDIC coverage	$600,000

Interview with Richard Marston on International Investing

Finance professor, Richard Marston, has been teaching at the Wharton School, University of Pennsylvania since 1972. He is also Director, Weiss Center for International Financial Research and a member of the Board of Editors for *Journal of International Economics, Empirical Economics, Journal of Economic Literature, Journal of International Money and Finance* and *Japan and the World Economy*. Professor Marston shares his opinions on international investing, asset allocation, and economic and career trends for physicians.

16

Are stocks of U.S. multinational corporations good substitutes for foreign stocks — since you can get international exposure without a lot of the risks associated with international investing?

What you're really asking is this. If you invested in companies like Coca-Cola and Ford (which have extensive cash flows from overseas), is that a good substitute for investing some of your portfolio in foreign companies that are listed on foreign exchanges and have their headquarters abroad?

Here's my answer. More than 50 percent of the cash flow profits of many U.S. multinational companies come from overseas. In almost every case, despite the fact that these companies rely heavily on foreign markets and foreign operations, their stocks behave more like American stocks than they do foreign stocks. In order to be effective substitutes for foreign stocks, the domestic stocks of the multinational company you're interested in would have to be highly correlated to the stocks that they would replace in the portfolio. For example, Coca-Cola would have to be highly correlated with for example, European stocks.

When you actually do this statistical test, here's what you find: American multinational stocks are very highly correlated with the U.S. stock indexes such as the S&P, but have virtually no correlation at all with the foreign stocks they would replace in a portfolio. So the answer is basically that the substitution of U.S. multinational stocks for foreign stocks in a portfolio simply doesn't work. It doesn't give you the effect of diversification that you are looking for.

17

In your opinion, did Britain make the right decision to stay with the pound and reject the Euro?

I think Britain definitely made the wrong decision. The prime minister is in favor of joining the European Union, and I believe that eventually the British will get around to doing it. Here's why. First, London is the financial center of Europe. In the long term, it seems very difficult to imagine that London could remain so without sharing the European currency. Second, during times when the British currency appreciates against the Euro, it would lead to serious competitive problems for British exports. That has actually occurred during the past 18 months. As a result, British exports are suffering significantly against continental products. Third, Britain has, in the past, significantly benefited from foreign investment in Europe by Japanese and American firms who prefer to be located in an English-speaking country. Japanese firms have recently said that they have made decisions to locate their plants on the continent, rather than in Britain, primarily because the British pound is going to remain a separate currency. Together, these make a very compelling argument for why the British eventually are going to have to find a way to join the union.

18

Why do France and Germany have unemployment rates around 10 percent, more than double the U.S. unemployment rate?

The first (and main) reason is the restrictiveness of the labor markets in European countries (excluding Britain). These European countries have very expensive benefit plans. That means that the total compensation package for a worker is often significantly above the wage that the worker receives. In some countries, estimates are that in order to hire a worker for $40,000, you actually have to pay them a total compensation of $80,000. This is because benefit packages, which are required by law and are customary in these countries, plus labor market taxes add significantly to the cost of hiring.

Second, many of these countries have restrictions (either by law or through the influence of labor unions) that dictate the compensation that has to be given if you fire a worker — even when you are closing down a subsidiary. For example, in some countries, you might have to pay a whole year's salary if the worker has been working for you for several years. So the required compensation for layoffs is much higher than in the U.S. Since it's more expensive to hire and more expensive to fire employees, these European firms are less willing to hire additional marginal workers during an upturn in the economy. They would much prefer to give overtime work to their existing workforce.

19

What is investor home bias? What causes it?

Home bias is the tendency of all investors, whatever country, to tend to prefer their own country's stocks and bonds to other countries' stocks and bonds. In the U.S., even institutional investors have this home bias. U.S. corporate pension funds tend to have only 10-12 percent of their portfolios invested in foreign stocks. European corporate pension funds (for example, the British and Dutch ones) typically invest 25-30 percent of their portfolios outside those countries. But those countries are very small countries in terms of the size of their financial markets. So 25-30 percent percent is still a very small number.

Why do investors have a home bias? Well, that's a bit of a puzzle. We all tend to regard our own assets as being safer, but even when you take into account any currency fluctuations, it doesn't make any sense statistically to overemphasize domestic investments to the extent that we do in the U.S. I think that maybe a psychological barrier that causes us to feel more comfortable keeping our money at home rather than diversifying the portfolio into foreign markets.

20

When do you think the Japanese economy and the Japanese market will recover?

The Japanese economy has had a series of false starts in the last 10 years. Each one caused the economy to improve because of government spending — and we're talking about rather extraordinary increases in government spending on what we would call infrastructure projects to try to get the economy started. Every time government spending starts to decline, the rest of the economy doesn't make up the difference and the economy falls back into a slow period. Recently, in the third and fourth quarters of 1999, the Japanese economy once again fell into a recession.

Now, what is the problem in Japan? The problem is basically that the consumer sector has not chosen to start spending to the extent that they had in the 1960s, 1970s and 1980s. They are emphasizing saving. They are very worried about the economy and as a result, they're cutting back on their expenditures. I believe that the Japanese economy will not recover on a sustainable basis until the Japanese consumer begins to spend at a more normal clip. So, the key to watch in Japan is consumer sentiment and consumer spending. Only when that turns up in a sustained way will the economy recover and start getting back on its old growth path.

21

Your daughter is currently in her second year of medical school. How do you feel about career prospects in medicine?

I'm not an expert in this area. Clearly there has been a downshift in income prospects for most medical doctors. I realize there are some specialties that are relatively immune to this trend, but there has been a definite shift down in terms of prospects compared with when I was a college student. That has its good and bad aspects. One good aspect is that people entering the medical field are very much committed to being doctors and are contributing to society in this way. Whereas when I was a college student, the income motive was clearly part of the picture for some people entering medicine. So that's a good thing. The bad aspect is that society as a whole responds to economic incentives, and you get more brilliant people entering the medical field by providing sufficient financial incentives.

This significant decline in physicians' income will be a drawback for society over the long run. You get motivated people, but you might not get as many talented people that you might have gotten in an earlier generation. My impression is that the smart people that want to make a good income often go into consulting or investment banking, whereas 20 or 30 years ago they might have gone into medicine. That on balance is not a good thing for medicine. On the other hand from knowing my daughter and her many friends who are in the medical field, I feel there are really some wonderful people entering the medical field despite the fact that the prospects of future income are much less than they have been in the past.

22

What influence does day trading have on the stock market. And is it growing?

I think that day trading is definitely something that has grown over the past 12 to 18 months. That increase is part of a phenomenon I regard as a temporary shift towards growth stocks and high technology stocks, which encourages day trading. Plus, technology that allows people to day-trade has improved so much. I think we have already seen the shakeout of this phenomenon with the fall of the NASDAQ.

Also, the notion that people would quit their regular jobs to spend their time day trading is close to insane. You have to remember that the business of managing financial assets is extremely difficult, and that the average manager of a mutual fund (who is clearly better informed and better trained than the average day-trader) under-performs the index.

There are managers out there that have impressive records over the long run, but they tend to be in the minority. They're the Peter Lynches of the world. If this is the case, how can we expect the average day-trader or even talented day-traders to consistently make money in the stock market selecting stocks? Many of these day-traders are not trained as analysts. As a result, I am not at all surprised to hear stories, many anecdotal stories, of significant losses on the part of day-traders.

Investing is a difficult business. I know an awful lot about investing, but I don't select individual stocks for my own portfolio. Occasionally I'll buy an individual stock, but I leave the bulk of my portfolio in the hands of full-time professionals who do the selection of stocks for me. That is what the investment industry does well and I would rather leave that to a professional.

I am definitely negative on day trading. This kind of phenomena starts to rise in a bull market, as you get towards the tail end of a bull market. The emphasis on individuals buying — and spending a lot of time buying — individual stocks occurred in the late 1960s and early 1970s. We all know what that leads to in the long run.

23

What is your opinion of index funds versus actively managed mutual funds?

There are some actively managed funds that have consistently beaten the index funds. The burden of proof is on the active manager. What investors really need is a lot of help in selecting these good mutual fund managers. In many firms, the financial consultants have access to research on which managers have done well in the past. I think investors should take advantage of this research to determine which of the active managers have done well in the past.

If you don't use this approach, I believe that, on average, just throwing a dart at a dartboard and choosing a manager, you're probably just as well off or better off with an index fund. As you get beyond the large cap U.S. stock mutual funds, I think it is increasingly important to get an active manager rather than go with an index fund because these markets tend to be relatively inefficient. The more you move away from large cap U.S. stocks into foreign stocks, small cap stocks or micro cap stocks in the United States, an active manager will benefit you more.

24

How will the U.S. handle the projected shortfalls of Social Security and Medicare?

I think the Social Security and Medicare shortfalls will lead to very significant burdens on the younger generation in the long run. The politicians in Washington do not want to address these problems because they are such unpopular subjects. If you talk to people in their twenties, like my daughters and their friends, you find a great deal of skepticism about the long-run viability of the Social Security system—let alone the Medicare system — which is in even worse shape. With the demographics that are occurring over time, we have virtually no control over it except to the extent that we allow increased immigration of skilled workers. This demographic trend will mean that eventually we are going to have a significantly smaller working population to support the Social Security and Medicare systems.

Both of these systems are pay-as-you-go systems. They require that you have a work force to pay the taxes in order to provide the retirement for the current retirees. Most Americans do not understand a pay-as-you-go system. They think they put their money in Social Security and then they take that money out at a later date when they retire. In fact, the money is put into Social Security and is not saved in any meaningful sense. In the long run, Americans are going to be facing these very significant demographic trends that will start to occur as soon as the baby boomer bulge in the population begins to retire within the next 10 years. Therefore, we are going to need major changes to face these challenges. One possibility that has already been partly implemented by law is raising the retirement age. I believe this makes a lot of sense, because the average 65 or 70-year-old is far healthier than he or she was 30 or 40 years ago. Second, we are going to have to either raise taxes on Social Security or cut benefits.

The sooner we start to modify the system, the better off we will be. This is a very difficult challenge facing politicians. In a recent presidential campaign, one of the candidates talked about introducing a very modest private insurance scheme within Social Security and was hammered by his opponent. Americans want to stick their heads in the sand, not worry about this; they think somehow it will be fixed later. My feeling is the sooner we do something meaningful about this the better. The Social Security Commission that was formed a few years ago developed excellent recommendations but once again they were not able to agree on these recommendations because our country is so split on these matters. This is a very important issue and will have a major impact but we may not be able to face up to it as a country until later in this century.

25

Do you think the Federal Reserve Chairman is overreacting to the wealth effect?

Overall, I think the Chairman Greenspan is doing a terrific job – and has been since he was appointed in 1987. Both Volcker and Greenspan have been very effective in getting this country out of the inflation messes we had in the late 1970s and early 1980s.

In terms of the current economic environment, I believe Chairman Greenspan is focusing more on the excess spending in the economy that has occurred over the past few years. How do we measure this excess spending? You measure it by comparing it to our output. The current level of spending of this economy as a whole is significantly greater than its output. How do we know that as economists? The excess spending shows up in the trade deficit or, more accurately, in the current account deficit of the balance of payments.

The extent that we spend more than we produce has to spill over into foreign goods or demand for foreign goods. In 1999, we had excess spending of more than $300 billion. That has fueled growth that has exceeded five percent recently. This is not sustainable in the long run. If we keep it up, we are going to inevitably end up in higher inflation and, also inevitably, the Federal Reserve is going to have to slam on the brakes. Greenspan is trying to prevent this scenario by slowly reducing spending by raising interest rates.

I applaud the effort even though it hurts those of us who have floating rate mortgages. I also applaud his effort to try to slow down the economy and try to get a soft landing so that we can grow at two to three percent rather than five percent. This is sustainable in the long run. Greenspan has been able to do this in the past (as in 1994) but it is a very difficult thing to do. The danger is in overdoing and driving the economy into recession. This is not a science but an art on how to slow down the economy. Greenspan has done a terrific job in the past and I believe he is better able than anyone else to help us achieve a soft landing.

26

You mentioned our massive trade deficits. What effect will these massive trade deficits have?

The main effect over the next five to 10 years will be on the value of the dollar. Currently, we have an overly strong dollar compared to the Euro. It is probably about 20-25 percent overvalued. This has happened in the past and it is no cause for alarm, but what we have to do is recognize this situation as investors. Right now, the dollar is unusually strong.

Foreigners are unusually enthusiastic about the American economy, and that has allowed us to run a trade deficit of $300 billion.

What we have are foreigners who are willing to invest in our assets and to allow us to borrow through their investments in stocks or bonds or invest in our bank deposits. It allows us to borrow so that we can overspend in the short run, but eventually this turns around. The dollar will start falling and, as a result, there will be a self-correcting mechanism. One of the reasons why our trade deficit is so large is because the dollar is overvalued and this makes it more difficult for U.S. exporters to sell abroad.

It also makes it much more attractive to buy from abroad. American tourists are having a wonderful time in Europe because prices are much cheaper than they will be in the long run. Also American consumers are attracted to foreign goods because they are currently very cheap. Eventually the dollar will fall, and that has an implication for investing to the extent that you have foreign investments. These foreign investments will benefit from a falling dollar or decline in the value of the dollar because it will raise the value of the foreign currency investments measured in dollar terms. This is the kind of self-correcting mechanism that all economies have, and I think this will be the effect of these huge deficits. These deficits will come down when spending is at a more leisurely pace because of Fed action and as the dollar declines in value. We do not know when this will occur (I'm talking about a five to 10 year period) but, in the short run, we cannot predict currencies.

27

Some futurists and demographers predict that our economy and markets will slow down and possibly go into recession as the baby boomers start to retire at the end of this decade. What is your opinion?

I think that demographics always have an effect on financial markets. Remember the boom in real estate in the late 1970s and 1980s? Part of that was an inflation phenomena and part of that was that baby boomers needed additional housing. Demographics will clearly have an effect over the next 10 to 15 years, because this huge bulge in the population is now in the process of desperately saving for retirement. The baby boomers have not done a very good job of saving for retirement over the past 20 years, but now they realize they want to retire (some want to retire early) and yet they haven't accumulated enough assets. As a result, some experts in the market believe that one of the reasons the stock market is doing so well lately is because so many of the baby boomers are saving and investing in stocks. As the baby boomers retire, I would expect them to reduce their investments in stocks. What I think will happen is a lot of different influences will affect the stock market. It's not just one influence (i.e., the demographics of baby boomers), but other factors — such as the state of the economy and level of interest rates.

The first factor is that we move towards the end of this decade, it is true that some of these baby boomers will begin retiring. On the other hand, other baby boomers will be desperately saving for retirement because baby boomer population will start retiring in significant numbers in the next decade. As they save and invest, they may be canceling out some of the reductions in portfolios that are happening with the newly retired baby boomers.

The second factor is that as the baby boomer population gets closer to retirement, there will be greater emphasis on good retirement planning. I believe that good retirement planning requires that retired people keep significant portions of their portfolios invested in the stock market. I think as we go forward, more and more baby boomers will realize that the day of retirement is not a day when you completely revise your investment philosophy. The typical retiree who retires in his or her early 60s has a life expectancy of more than 20 more years. With such a life expectancy, the big danger is that the assets you accumulate before retirement will not be sufficient to allow you a comfortable retirement throughout your lifetime.

For this reason, I think there will be an increasing emphasis on significant investment in the equity markets even in retirement years. I don't believe the baby boomers will continue to invest heavily in the equity markets until the latter part of this decade — and then start dumping their stocks upon retirement. I think it is going to be a much smoother process, with a lot of other factors influencing investment in the stock market.

28

Investors who have been well diversified through asset allocation over the past five years have not done as well as the S&P 500 index fund. Are you still recommending asset allocation to investors?

Yes. I think the last five years especially favored U.S. large cap stock index funds. This was an extraordinary time for this sector; in fact this sector had its best performance in U.S. history. During this period, the best strategy would have been to keep all of your assets in the U.S. stock market — specifically in the large company stocks represented by the Russell 1000 or S&P 500. With the benefit of hindsight, that would have been the best thing to do.

On the other hand, if we look into the past, there are other periods when the best thing to do would have been to put all your money into small cap U.S. stocks. This happened five years in a row in the early 1980s. The best thing to do in the late 1980s was to put all of your money into foreign stocks. There is always a best market in this world and it just so happens that in the last five years, the best market has been large cap U.S. stocks. Is that going to be the case all the time?

My strong conviction is that it is not going to be the case. Over time, there are going to be other markets that are going to outperform the large cap U.S. stocks. The only way for someone who is serious about building up capital for retirement or for some other long term goal is to invest on a balanced basis in a diversified portfolio — taking advantage of the long-term benefits of asset allocation. Asset allocation will reduce the risk of the portfolio and will provide a long-term return high enough to provide for wealth accumulation for satisfactory retirement.

29

Do you feel Americans are over-invested in the tech sector?

I think over the last couple of years the tech sector has had a wonderful run. If you look at the whole growth stock sector, which include other industry other than tech and is characterized by very high price earnings ratios, the last two years have been the best years we have had. During this period, tech stocks have been the leaders. If you had loaded up your portfolio in tech stocks, you would have done extraordinarily well.

The problem is that, there is always some sector of the stock market that does extraordinarily well. The best way to make sure you are not going to be accumulating wealth in the long run at the pace you desire, is to load up on one particular sector. History tells that if one sector performs well for a few years, it's going to be followed up another sector significantly outperforming it. For example, in the early 1970s, the stocks of the era; the Polaroids, Xeroxes and so on fascinated investment professionals. And a lot of people recommended investing in the so-called "nifty-fifty" stocks over the next few years after this recommendation came out. Then the market completely shifted and those who were invested in the high tech stocks lost a significant amount on the stock market.

I think Americans are overemphasizing tech. It is true that we're in the middle of a significant tech revolution. We've seen this so many times in U.S. history; we've had breakthroughs in technology which have lead to increases in our growth rate and so on. We're in the middle of a breakthrough. The question is whether or not the stock market has way overextended; way beyond whatever real phenomena has taken place in the high tech area. I believe that is the case.

When you have price earnings ratios that are way above 100, you have to start to worry about whether or not the stock market has priced in what could happen over the next 20 years but also some fanciful things that could happen over the next 50 years. I think indeed, Americans have over emphasized tech investments. Recently, they have seen these stocks can go down just as rapidly as the went up.

30

What is your opinion of the consolidation of stock exchanges and currencies?

The consolidation of stock exchanges is occurring a great deal in Europe. I think the catalyst for this is the common European currency: the Euro. There is now a system for national stock markets in virtually every country of Western Europe. That is not viable in the long run, since we're seeing such increasing integration of the European economy.

Each of the stock markets has stayed within national boundaries — unlike the bond market, which is now centered in London.

The stock markets are now attempting to merge. The most exciting proposed merger is between the London and Frankfurt exchanges. Under the proposal, the main stock market will move to London, and both German and British stocks will be listed there. The NASDAQ-type market will stay in Frankfurt — and so a lot of the exciting growth will occur in the Frankfurt-type part of the market. There will be a merger of the two markets with a common board of directors.

A merger is also taking place between the French market and some of the other markets in Western Europe. I think this trend toward mergers and integration will make it easier for investors (particularly institutional investors) to carry out trade. In the future, I believe this trend will help the retail investors as well. Currently, it is the institutional investors that are pushing these mergers across the board.

31

You mentioned that the bond market is being centralized in London. The spreads or difference between the bid and the ask prices for European bonds have gone through significant changes, haven't they?

Yes, the spreads on European government bonds (which is the most liquid part of the bond market), have gone through significant changes. The bond market has gone from having eleven or twelve different locations to having one — in London. It's an electronic market so it is a little difficult to talk about it being located in a particular city — but the center of the market is in London. Most of the traders now live in London.

As a result of this consolidation, the spreads have been cut (according to Salomon Brothers by as much as two-thirds). They are almost down to American levels. We are ending up with a market almost as liquid as the U.S. Treasury market. This is an exciting change; one which in the long run will encourage the development of the corporate bond market in Europe to an extent that they never have seen before.

32

Is there anything else you would recommend to physicians?

I think the main thing for physicians to realize is that you are going to accumulate capital and planning for retirement because you probably can't keep up the physical pace past your mid-sixties. How do you secure a reasonable retirement? Very early on, you must get serious about the investment process and make sure you get good professional advice. This may mean paying a fee to a consultant to look over your portfolio to make sure that you have the right mix of assets and then sticking to a plan. Once you've made the plan when you are forty years old, add assets as rapidly as you can to the retirement plan — as well as outside of the retirement plan. You need to take the investment process seriously.

My impression is that a lot of professionals — doctors and lawyers included — get involved in harebrained schemes. As a result, they don't stick to a long-term plan for investing. I think a sensible conservative plan that includes significant, broadly diversified investment in the stock market, plus other investments — perhaps in real estate, perhaps in fixed income. It should be a broadly diversified portfolio that has been designed by a professional consultant. I think this is the way to go for that long-term goal of wealth accumulation and this will make all the difference in the world.

The last few years has proven this. The difference between a 50 or 55-year-old who invests long-term during this boom period and a 50 or 55-year-old that has been dabbling with their investments on their own is monumental. Good long-term strategies have paid off in the past — and I believe they will in the future.

This is my one piece of advice. Get some professional advice and stick with a plan. If you do, you'll have that kind of comfortable retirement that we all dream about.

33

What would you recommend to high school students who are preparing for college?

Think broadly about what type of education you want. Don't become too narrow too quickly. Try to get a broad background in the arts and sciences, as well as in economics, in business or in whatever you choose. Think broadly in terms of career choices because the job that you get right after college is not that important to your long-term future. You have to think about where you want to be when you are 30 or 40 years old. This may require you to think of programs that may not have a direct career path. In the long run, these courses and programs might make you a much better person — and much broader individual. You have to keep your options open. Think long-term about what kind of person you want to be. And take courses that are intellectually exciting.

Interview with Jeremy Siegel on Investing for Long Term Growth

When the stock market experiences dramatic volatility causing angst among investors, you'll frequently see Professor Jeremy J. Siegel being interviewed on major TV networks explaining the mysteries of the economy and stock market. Since 1976, Siegel has been a finance professor at the Wharton School, University of Pennsylvania. He is the author of the best selling book, *Stocks For The Long Run, A Guide to Selecting Markets for Long-Term Growth* (Irwin Publishing).

34

During the 1990s, stock prices more than tripled. Has this bull market attracted record numbers of Americans who, thinking these returns are the norm, have become equity investors?

This is definitely our biggest concern — that investors will take the last 10 years as typical. But, actually, the great boom began in 1982. We are talking about almost 20 years when returns have been about twice the long run average. I do think many Americans do believe that they will be able to get 15, 20 or 25 percent yearly return, but there is a lot of literature and a lot of advisors telling them that only 10 percent is the long-run return on the market.

35

Do American investors have unreasonable expectations?

Some do, particularly in the high tech areas, which have seen spectacular gains recently. But I think that a lot of investors who are investing for the long term are more realistic about the more moderate gains they can expect to see.

36

Is high inflation over?

I think there's a good chance that the risk of having the kind of double-digit inflation that we experienced in the 70s is over. The central banks have learned their lesson about how to avoid those mistakes. However, I do believe that inflation in the neighborhood of four or five percent (which would be considered high by today's standards; certainly not high by post-war standards) is certainly possible within the next decade or so.

37

Do you feel the market or certain of its sectors are overvalued?

I do feel, despite the Internet revolution, that Internet stocks are overvalued. Recently, I have been concerned about such fine companies as Cisco, Sun Micro, Nortel, that provide the backbone for the Internet. These companies also are overvalued and by that I mean having price earnings ratios greater than 100. I can understand more reasonable valuations of 50, 60, 70 and even 80 do not scare me but valuations over 100 do not have any historical precedence.

38

What's in store for Social Security, Medicare and the national debt? Are we really going to solve these problems?

It's quite remarkable — the turn-around that our fiscal policy has taken over the last five years. And now the congressional budget office is predicting that much of the national debt in the hands of the public will be eliminated within ten to fifteen years. Part of this is certainly dependent upon fiscal discipline. We are already above spending limits in the last year or so. We must reassert our fiscal discipline. Even with these surpluses, Social Security may be in difficulty over the long run. And with our increasing life expectancy,

Medicare is another persistent problem. So even though the outlook is much better than we have seen for many decades, we have not solved Social Security and Medicare for the long run.

39

How will the Internet affect the U.S. economy? The global economy?

The Internet is a communications revolution. It's already affecting our economy, most noticeably in the capital markets, but even more immediately in how easy it's made it for us to communicate. This will benefit communication between individuals, between individuals and businesses, and between businesses. This last one promises large and important savings for consumers. The ability of the global economy to be captured in the Internet and for communications to be readily available to all participants immediately is also going to lead to a great increase in discoveries, improvements and technological advancements. I believe these positive developments make the future appear very bright.

40

Have American investors become less interested in dividend growth and more interested in total returns because of tax policy changes?

Taxation is one reason that dividend yields are down. Certainly we understand that tax on capital gains is less than on ordinary income, but I think there are other reasons that investors have become less interested in dividend growth. I think it's that investors are more in tune to growth in capital gains as the biggest source of retirement income. More and more, retirees are liquidating their capital gains as sources of spending money rather than trying to keep capital in tact and spending out of the dividends. The latter method, favored by the older generation, has a degree of artificiality to it because it is dependent upon the dividend policies of individual firms. I think this lessened interest in dividend growth is more of a change in the way investors perceive the growth of wealth rather than just the influence of taxation policy.

41

What will be the long-term effect of our current trade imbalance?

Our trade imbalance leads to our current account imbalance. This means that foreigners are accumulating more American assets than Americans are accumulating foreign assets. Since the U.S. currently has the most productive economy in the world, there's no real concern about this problem. Foreigners seem more than willing to hold our assets and even raise our dollar exchange rates. However, if negative political or economic events do occur in the U.S., that dollar overhang will worsen the trade imbalance problem. This could cause sharp depreciation in the value of the dollar on foreign exchange markets, which would raise the price of imported goods — particularly oil.

42

What changes will be created by the communications revolution?

The communications revolution is well on its way not just for individuals, but for businesses too. Perhaps more important is that virtually anybody can now be part of the collective body of knowledge and learning that constitutes human advancement. Many countries have very bright people, but they haven't been able to go to schools or to associate with individuals that can bring out their intelligence or their ability to advance humankind. I believe the Internet will reveal many of these individuals, and spur worldwide technological change.

43

What are the pros and cons of mergers of these global giants?

These mergers are to be expected. They appear to be large and in absolute value, they are. But, relative to the size of our capital markets, they are not that large. The value of large companies today (as a fraction of the total market value) is actually less than it was 30 years ago. We will see continued consolidation; however, this does not mean that the government has to be constantly on the lookout for combinations that stifle competition and prevent the best prices from reaching consumers.

44

Is the equity premium or the difference between expected equity returns and government bond yields being reduced? How will this affect investors and corporations?

I have studied this extensively. I have written articles on the shrinking equity premium. The difference between the return on stocks and bonds will go down in the future. It's not that I believe stock returns will be lower; it's that bond returns will be higher. We see bond returns now four or five percent above the rate of inflation. These are very high by historical standards. Index bonds that are protected from inflation are also yielding in excess of four percent. The reason for the decline in the equity premium is more because fixed income yields are going up than because future stock returns are going down.

45

Do you notice any significant change in the students you teach at Wharton these days? Have their attitudes changed towards being an entrepreneurs v. managers of Fortune 100 companies?

I am very fortunate here at Wharton, because we attract the very best students. Overall, I have been very impressed. But it is most certainly true that a shift is well underway; students are now more likely to become entrepreneurs, not managers of Fortune 100 companies. The technological communication and Internet revolutions have made the prospect of joining young fast growing firms very attractive. The older firms are most certainly losing out in their recruiting efforts among the best business schools in the country.

46

What changes do you see occurring among universities over the next decade? What changes would you like to see?

I believe the greatest change will be what we've come to call "distance learning." Because of the Internet and communication revolutions, the ability to transmit knowledge and information in places other than a formal classroom has increased significantly. It's my belief that students may be taking courses from the best professors from around the world — no matter what university they attend — and then only meet in discussion sessions among their fellow students. Universities won't disappear, but they will be very different types of learning centers than they are today.

47

What advice would you give to high school students and their parents about making the most of their college experience?

I have always felt that there are many complex features of the college experience. Students must visit their prospective colleges and then trust their own instincts. No one can really tell you what's best for you except you yourself. Go to classes, look at dormitories, look at students, talk to students, look at catalogs. If you do a thorough job, my feeling is that the right answer will come to you naturally.

48

What advice would you give to your students as they prepare for graduation and get ready to pursue a career?

I believe that the most important aspect of pursuing a successful career is selecting a field or area you really enjoy. Many students believe that they should like a certain area or they have been taught they should like a certain area either from their parents or their peers. You have to follow what you really enjoy, because you'll find out you do best in what you enjoy. You learn better. You learn faster. We economists would say that is pursuing your comparative advantage. What you think best about, what you enjoy learning, those are the areas you should pursue.

49

Recently there have been several books written predicting that the Dow Jones Industrial Average will soar to 36,000 this decade and beyond. You have been quoted as being very skeptical and believing a recession or economic slowdown will probably happen. Please explain.

The Dow 36,000 book written by a close friend of mine, Kevin Hassick and James Glassman, actually is based on the work in my book, *Stocks For The Long Run, A Guide to Selecting Markets for Long-Term Growth*. However, they take my conclusions to an extreme. I explain that stocks are no more risky than bonds in the long run. Mr. Hassick and Mr. Glassman then say that stocks should return no more than bonds in the long run. If you go through their math, that means that stocks should rise threefold from their current level. That's where I disagree. I think that stock returns might go down slightly in the future, but I believe bond returns, will go up much more. So we don't need stock returns to rise so dramatically to reduce them to the bond return. As far as recession or economic slowdown, I would say that the odds are that we have not conquered the business cycle. However, there are also persuasive reasons to believe that whatever cyclical fluctuations we will have in the future will be less severe than we have had in the past.

50

What are the strengths of our economy?

Our biggest strength is the growth of productivity, which is unprecedented eight, nine, 10 years into a business cycle. The communications and technological revolution has set in motion forces that have exhilarated productivity levels to levels we've only seen in the 1960s. And there is some belief that we may even go beyond those levels.

51

Where are we most vulnerable?

Despite our tremendous gains in productivity, the soaring stock market spending has been rising even more rapidly. As a result, we have seen a depletion of the pool of available workers that can provide us with this increased output and this is where we are most vulnerable. Therefore, there are signs that the economy must cool somewhat to avoid imbalances developing that could put an end to this remarkable economic expansion.

52

What advice do you have for investors?

There are two pieces of advice. The first is to keep your expectations in line with the long-run reality. My work suggests that, in the long run, stock returns are seven percent after inflation (which would be something in the neighborhood of nine or 10 percent before inflation). That's long run. The double-digit gains that we've seen over the last decade are not normal. I would certainly also advise diversification. I know that's not exciting, but it reduces risk dramatically and (certainly for long term investors) has proven to be one of the most beneficial ways to help you increase your wealth.

53

Any other comments?

We live in a remarkable era. The promise of technology is greater than it has been for many, many decades. But we must remember that all the gains from this communications revolution will not reside only with corporations and shareholders in the form of profits. History has showed us that most technology gains move down to the level of individuals and consumers. They are the ones that gain through lower prices of the goods that they buy. However exciting these technologies may be, they don't automatically translate to huge profits.

Chapter 2
Economic Influences

In spite of the fact that our economy is currently the envy of other nations —with unemployment around four percent and inflation less than two percent — approximately 1.4 million Americans filed for personal bankruptcy last year. Credit card debt is subsidizing many individuals' life styles. More than two-thirds of Americans do not or cannot pay their MasterCard, Visa or charge card bills in full when they receive them. Many simply make the minimum allowable payment and permit the 18 percent plus annual interest rate to compound.

Harry Dent was one of the earliest to recognize one of the most powerful influences in our economy — the spending wave of the 76 million baby boomers. He wrote about it in his best-selling books, *The Great Boom Ahead* and *The Roaring 2000s*. Dent graciously shares his views on these economic influences in an interview following this chapter.

54

The dramatic rise in the stock market during the past decade was partially fueled by the baby boomers. Will the stock market drop as the boomers begin to retire during the next decade and start liquidating their investments?

No. Retiring baby boomers (the name describes the approximately 76 million Americans born between 1946 and 1964), like all retirees, need to plan to triple their incomes during retirement to keep ahead of inflation and maintain their purchasing powers. Individuals planning on retiring in their 50s need to quadruple their incomes during retirement. Since fixed income investments lack protection against inflation, baby boomers will need to keep a substantial part of their portfolios in stocks to stay ahead of inflation.

55

Many baby boomers have not saved nor invested enough for their retirements. What do you think will happen to them when they want to retire?

It is estimated that two-thirds of American baby boomers are failing to plan properly for their retirements. Because of this, they face three challenges. First, they face being forced to work past the normal retirement age. Second, they face not being able to enjoy their current life styles once they do retire. And third and most important, they run the risk of outliving their money.

56

I am familiar with the problems that inflation causes retirees, like outliving your money because of rising expenses. Lately I have been hearing a lot about deflation. What problems are caused by deflation?

Deflation creates a very difficult business environment, characterized by dropping prices, eroding gross margins and declining profits. As a result, layoffs occur. Businesses shrink and their suppliers' businesses shrink, which causes further layoffs and more unemployment. This overall slowdown affects corporate earnings and creates a decline in common stock prices as well as real estate prices.

57

With the scares in the Russian, Asian and Latin American stock markets — and recently in our own stock market — what is to prevent America from having a 1929-type crash and depression?

We and our policy makers have learned some lessons from the Crash of '29. Since then, safety nets have been put in place — like unemployment insurance and deposit insurance for bank accounts — to help protect us from severe economic and market shocks. And watchdog agencies like the Federal Reserve and the Securities and Exchange Commission (SEC) have been established to protect investors.

And remember that, during the 1920s, widespread speculation was sanctioned, which meant that investors could leverage just $10,000 to purchase $100,000 in securities (a margin rate of 10 percent). Today the Federal Reserve controls margin rates; the rate is 50 percent.

During the Great Depression of the 1930s, our government kept interest rates high in order to try to balance the budget. This stifled borrowing — both by businesses and consumers. Today, when our economy slows, the Federal Reserve lowers interest rates and increases the money supply to stimulate borrowing by businesses and consumers. Our government also tries to stimulate the economy by increasing spending (this is called deficit financing) to increase purchasing power and create jobs.

58

Is there really a federal budget surplus?

Let me put it this way. If Social Security revenue and expenditures were separated from the federal budget, the $124 billion federal budget surplus in 1999 would have disappeared since Social Security surplus was $125 billion. Several senators (from both parties), when interviewed on CNN just after a recent election, said they would sponsor legislation segregating Social Security from general revenue and expenditures. That way, "Americans would get a true picture of our budget surplus/deficit."

59

What is the January effect phenomena?

The January effect triggers the January stock market rally. Because of the December selling for tax reasons and the need for institutions to clean their balance sheets (portfolio window dressing), stock prices are artificially depressed at year-end. These artificially depressed stock prices create buying opportunities and historically stocks (especially small cap stocks) have risen from the last day of trading in December through the fourth trading day of January. This rise in small cap stocks during this period is called the January effect.

60

Since 1999 is a year before a presidential election, how does the stock market perform during pre-election years?

This year looks good! Since 1940, pre-election years have been by far the best performing years for the market. Realizing the past performance is no indication for future results, the numbers for the past 50-plus years for the Standard & Poor 500 Index with dividends are:

Pre-election year average .... + 21.05 percent
Election year average .... +12.40 percent
Post-election year average .... + 7.81 percent
Mid-term election year average ...... +10.23 percent

Note: The S&P 500 gained almost 20 percent in 1999.

61

I have a serious cash flow problem in my two-year-old medical practice caused by delays in getting paid by Medicare and third party payers. Any tips for speeding up payments?

Several local physicians commented the quickest way to get paid by Medicare is through electronic filing. Another physician mentioned that contacting your state Insurance Commissioner about insurance companies flagrantly past due in reimbursements would force payment of these overdue claims.

62

Isn't the Internet revolutionizing the way we do business?

Yes, the Internet is having and will have a profound effect and influence on our economy and our lives. Before the Internet, most retailers could attract only customers nearby unless they had branches and/or offered mail order catalogs. Now, individual manufacturers, retailers or wholesalers in remote locations can broadcast their offerings on the Internet. These offerings are now easily accessible to any domestic/foreign business or consumer who clicks on to its website.

The Internet is also eliminating channels of distribution between manufacturers and consumers. For example, Dell and Gateway sell specially built computers directly to businesses and individuals. This eliminates the extra cost of housing sample computers and inventory in thousands of retail locations. It also eliminates the need to mark down inventories no longer offering the latest bells and whistles. Transporting and warehousing costs of finished products between distributors, wholesalers and retailers are also eliminated, as well as the expense of printing and mailing millions of flyers and catalogs.

63

Is the mania over Internet stocks justified?

David Blitzer, chief economist and chairman of Standard & Poor's Selection Committee for the S&P 500, was asked recently if Internet stocks are overrated. He replied, "Yes, they are. Moreover, each one is priced like it is going to be the whole Internet, and they cannot all be the whole Internet." The exploding market capitalization of Internet companies such as Amazon.com (which has not as yet earned any profit, and which exceeds that of Borders and Barnes & Noble combined or Sears), has fundamental and technical analysts looking on in disbelief. Others have compared this buying frenzy for stocks.com to the 16th Century tulip mania in Holland, which drove the prices of tulip bulbs to astronomical levels and precipitated a price crash. I believe disappointed investors will dump overvalued Internet stocks that fail to meet revenue and/or earnings projections. This will result in major declines in share prices of these Internet stocks.

64

I'm a 62-year-old computer illiterate physician. I realize the Internet is not going away as a passing fad and I need to learn how to use it. How can I learn how to use the Internet?

An easy, free and painless way is have someone show you the "Learn the Internet" website at http://www.learnthenet.com. You'll find an easy-to-follow guide and tutorial in English, French, German, Spanish and Italian. Another option is to hire a teenage relative who enjoys surfing the web and have him or her teach you. In addition to learning how to best use the Internet, you'll provide a wonderful boost to a young person's self-esteem.

65

I've had a successful medical practice in a major metropolitan area for almost 23 years. In the last three years my annual income has dropped about 30 percent because of a loss of revenue to managed care. How widespread is this problem?

Very widespread. Managed care has dramatically changed the health care industry, according to MD Career Net (website:mdintellinet.com), a healthcare placement and consulting firm established by Dr. Gigi Hirsch. She was a psychiatry instructor at Harvard Medical School (1992-1997). She says, "Physicians currently represent a profession in crisis" and estimates that there is a surplus of 100,000-150,000 physicians in the U.S. today. Surveys reveal that more than 30 percent of physicians either would not recommend a medical career for their children or would not pursue one given the chance to do it again. Dr. Hirsch is also a consultant to hundreds of physicians seeking to make non-clinical career transitions. Dr. Gigi Hirsch's interview is on page 177.

66

My wife and I are both doctors (general internist and family practice), and we are really feeling the crunch. We are very interested in new opportunities of any kind. We regret that, though we always wanted to be clinical doctors, conditions have deteriorated and we need to pursue non-clinical jobs just to survive financially. What do you recommend?

I recommend that you explore opportunities with Dr. Gigi Hirsch at MDintellinet.com which was discussed in the prior question.

67

What does the S&P measure? What is the risk associated with investing in the S&P index?

The risk of investing in the S&P 500* is that it can give an inaccurate reading of the market. The Standard & Poor 500 (S&P 500) is a stock index often considered representative of the stock market in general. It is composed of the 500 largest U.S. public companies based on market capitalization (market price per share multiplied by the total number of outstanding shares). However, noted portfolio manager Philip Johanson recently published a study for 1998 disputing the notion that the S&P 500 is a broad-based index. He explains that each of the 500 stocks carry weighting measuring its total market cap divided by the total market cap of all 500 stocks. For example, Microsoft's market cap is $416 billion and the total market cap of all 500 stocks is $10.5 trillion. Therefore Microsoft represents 3.94 percent weighting in the S&P 500 index.

Johanson proves this is a top-heavy index as shown by the following cumulative weighting of each quintile. Dividing the top quintile by the five top stocks would comprise Microsoft, General Electric, Walmart, Merck and Intel. These five stocks impact this index as much as the bottom 300 stocks. He explains how nine out of every 10 stocks in this index could be up 15 percent and the overall index would only show a 1 percent increase. How? If the top 50 stocks declined 10 percent each, and the remaining 450 stocks increased 15 percent each, the overall index would only show a 1.08 percent increase.

Top	100 market capitalization stocks = 72.08%
2nd	100 market capitalization stocks = 14.85%
3rd	100 market capitalization stocks = 7.38%
4th	100 market capitalization stocks = 4.15%
5th	100 market capitalization stocks = 1.54%

The narrow band of supercharged large caps pushed some indices up dramatically in 1998 even though more stocks on the NYSE declined than increased in market price.

Standard & Poor's 500 Composite is an unmanaged but commonly used measure of common stock total return performance. It is not possible to invest in an index.

*S&P 500 is a trademark of Standard & Poor's Corporation.

68

What is the "wealth effect" that I hear keeps pushing up the stock market?

The wealth effect is an upward spiral of investor and consumer confidence, consumption, corporate earnings, and real estate and stock prices. It starts with the positive feeling Americans experience when they see their investment account values soar as the stock market rises and the value of their homes go up. Today, millions of Americans are feeling wealthier because their 401(k) or 403(b) or IRA statements are reaching new highs. This makes them feel more confident about their financial prospects even though they may be decades from retiring. Because of their increased net worth in their home equities and stock portfolios, investors feel richer and are willing to spend a greater share of their incomes on consumption instead of on saving. This increased consumption generally stimulates demand for corporate products and services, boosts sales revenues, profits and earnings per share. Improved corporate earnings drive up stock prices again adding to this "wealth effect." You need to realize that this "wealth effect" can also be negative and turn sour because of a downturn in the equity and/or real estate markets which can discourage consumption as investors feel poorer even though it's only on paper.

69

I know about the Baby Boomers and Generation X. What is Generation Y?

Generation Y is the 60 million members Americans aged seven through 22, the largest generation since the Baby Boomers (76 million). As you look at the chart of Live Births (measured by thousands) from 1959 through 1997, you'll see the spurt between 1977 and 1991. What implications does this spurt have? Well, if you have children applying for admission to competitive colleges and universities, the competition will continue to become harder over the next nine years as the pool of applicants increases.

Live Births (Thousands)

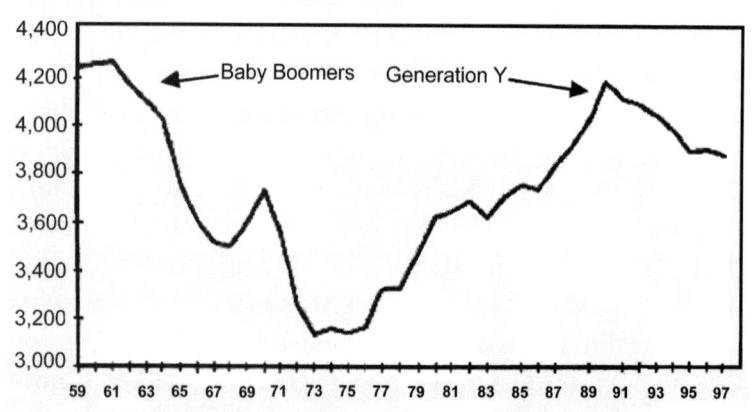

Source: U.S. Department of Health & Human Services

70

I'm baffled when market prices of companies reporting above or below average earnings remain virtually unchanged while unsubstantiated rumors about a company will drive its stock price to new highs or lows. Why?

Much of what happens on Wall Street baffles me too! Keep in mind that two major emotions are responsible for many short-term market swings; fear (especially on the way down) and greed (especially on the way up). Company earnings are the long-term driving force of the market. The stock market is more an anticipatory than reactionary market. Analysts may have estimated a company's quarterly earnings and its market price may reflect these estimates. Frequently, the markets have already factored in Federal Reserve rate hikes. So when they're finally announced, they've already been anticipated and therefore have no effect on current prices.

71

I have been in private practice as an internist in a major city for almost two years and realize that I am lousy at running a business. After all, I've been trained to administer to an individual's health needs — not trained to run a profitable practice. Any suggestions?

Usually, identifying a problem is the first major step towards solving it. So congratulations, you're on your way to a solution. I suggest that you develop a team of professionals to help you: an accountant, an attorney and a financial advisor. Many physicians ignore the importance of cash flow, generate massive account receivables, and then find themselves unable to pay current obligations like payroll and taxes. Why not talk to an experienced, successful physician and ask how he or she overcame these business challenges.

Here's some more food for thought. Can you evaluate what type of customer (patient) service you provide? Many physicians would refuse to do business with a firm that provided customer service as unsatisfactory as is found in their own practices. Imagine having to wait one hour or more to see an accountant, a banker, an attorney, a university president, a congressional representative or a corporate executive after having made a confirmed appointment. Patients resent having to wait hours to see a doctor after scheduling an appointment. How do you feel when you have to wait one hour in a plane waiting for take-off on a perfectly clear day? Many older patients also resent having a 30-year-old receptionist and physician address them by their first name while the physician expects to be called "Doctor" by his or her patients. Some doctors I spoke to said that third-party payers cause this deterioration of patient or customer service. Their patients are not their customers; they are not paid directly by their patients but by a third party. Plastic surgery for cosmetic reasons is an exception because the patient generally pays the plastic surgeon directly. The quality of customer (patient) service is exceptionally high for plastic surgery patients.

Some additional suggestions: How often do you personally check and update the magazines in your reading room? Do you have a comment form or suggestion form for patients to complete so that they know you care and do not take them for granted? Perception is reality.

72

When the market was going through considerable volatility, I became worried and sold my mutual fund because I thought it was going to continue dropping. Instead it shot up right after I sold it. Any suggestions for investors like me?

First rule: Don't beat yourself up on matters that are beyond your control!

Second rule: Do what you do best and hire the rest. Obviously, your strength is not in managing your portfolio during volatile periods. Use an investment professional who is objective, competent, has integrity, and with whom you relate. I don't know enough about your unique situation to give you specific advice but I realize you need help because you are a lot more aggressive in up markets than your risk tolerance permits during down times.

73

What is the difference among the various interest rates (the federal funds rate, prime rate and the discount rate) that are raised or lowered by the Federal Reserve?

Changing interest rates is one of the tools that the Federal Reserve uses to try to stimulate the economy (lowering rates) or reduce inflationary pressures (raising rates). The Federal Reserve can only change short-term rates such as the federal funds rate and the discount rate; banks set the prime rate. The federal funds rate is what banks charge each other for overnight borrowing. The discount rate is the rate charged by the Federal Reserve to its member banks when they borrow money using government securities as collateral. The prime rate also known as "the prime" is the interest rate banks charge for loans to their most creditworthy customers. The prime is considered a key benchmark because other rates are tied into it. For example, the interest rate for many credit cards (home equity loans and automobile leases) is based upon the prime rate plus a set number of percentage points.

Interview with Harry S. Dent, Jr. on Demographics

After having written the Answerman column for more than one year, the editors suggested I conduct interviews with experts whose advice would help our readers better understand the economy and how it affects their investments. The editor announced "we are turning the tables and letting the Answerman ask the questions." Our first interview was with Harry S. Dent, Jr. who offered his refreshingly positive insights into the financial future of physicians. Dent has been a frequent guest on *CNBC, PBS* and *Good Morning America* and been featured in the *Wall Street Journal, Barron's, Investor's Business Daily* and *Fortune*.

74

In 1993, you accurately predicted that the Dow Jones Industrial Average (Dow 30) would exceed 10,000 before the year 2000. In your current bestseller, "The Roaring 2000s," you predict that the Dow 30 will exceed 35,000 in the next decade. What is the basis for your predictions?

The most fundamental force driving the stock market is people and their predictable spending for major purchases like housing, furnishings, appliances and cars. Historically, the stock market has done well when a generation's spending peaks at age 46. There is a remarkable correlation between spending and stock market performance. Look at the graph of U.S. births Lagged for Peak Spending from 1955 to 2015; it shows the Dow 30's performance compared to spending. I believe that we are on the verge of the greatest stock market boom in history.

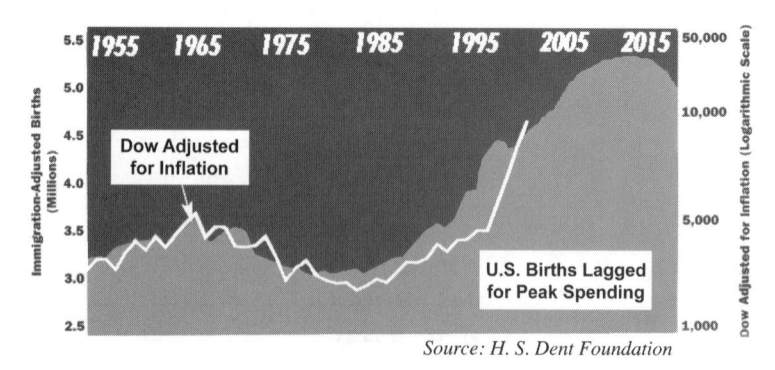

Source: H. S. Dent Foundation

75

What changes will occur in the health care industry in the next five to 10 to 20 years?

As information systems get better via the Internet and everything else, we see the system tilting more toward the patient and away from HMOs and managed care entities. Consumers will start to demand, and get, more choice. More and more, they'll say, "Well, it is fine for me to go to the HMO for minor health concerns, but if I have a heart problem or other major health threat, I'd rather have more choice and go to doctors of my own selection." Doctors will need to work closely with patients to understand their needs and help them find the right health care. Sometimes this may be an HMO; other times it may be the best surgeon or specialist. Doctors will need to work with their patients' health insurance companies to determine which coverage is best for their needs when it comes to catastrophic or basic coverage. Wherever there is a standardized procedure, patients need to know their doctors will help them get it at the lowest price through an HMO or other entity. We think the health care system is too top-down currently, and over the next 10 to 20 years consumers will demand more choice in health care and this will re-elevate the position of physicians.

76

Do you think the financial situation of physicians will change?

If you, as a physician, can become a trusted medical advisor to your patients and help them 1) take proactive preventative health initiatives where appropriate, and 2) get specialized services outside of the HMO when they need them, then you can get more control of your fees and add more value to your patients. Doctors will have to position themselves as trusted medical advisors rather than as HMO employees.

77

How long do you think it will take doctors to reposition themselves as trusted medical advisors?

I think it may take the next 10 to 20 years. In the next 10 years, it will follow the "S Curve" effect that I talk about in my book. That means that the smartest physicians will start to reposition themselves as trusted medical advisors, and others will begin to see the potential and follow. We see the same phenomena occurring with financial advisors. Already, a small minority of independent financial advisors are starting to integrate all services and position themselves as objective advisors who can help people make better choices. I see the same thing happening in health care — with maybe a five to 10 year lag.

The S-curve

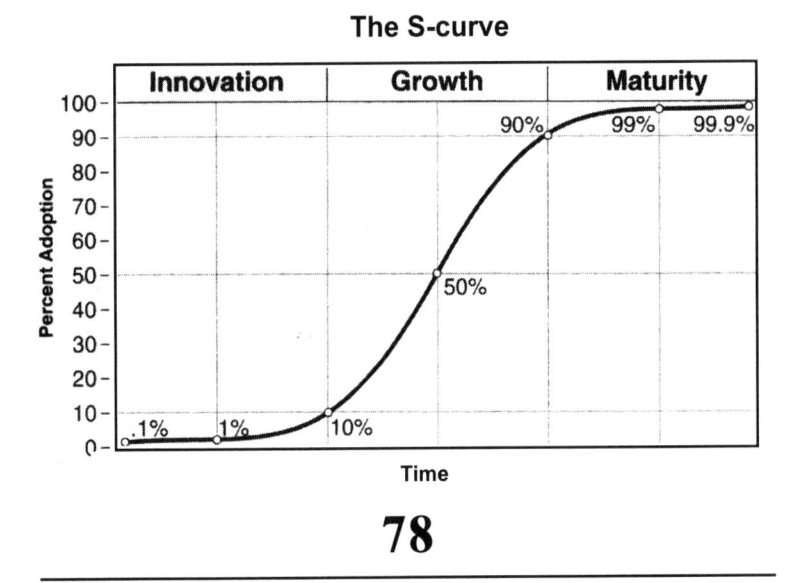

```
Percent Adoption
100 -
 90 -                                    90%    99%   99.9%
 80 -
 70 -
 60 -
 50 -                         50%
 40 -
 30 -
 20 -
 10 - .1%  1%   10%
  0 -
     Innovation │ Growth │ Maturity
              Time
```

78

Why should investors use financial advisors when there is an abundance of information on the Internet, at libraries, in books by authors like you, and in magazines such as this one? Why pay for something that is virtually free?

You may not need to, if you have the time to process all this information. The problem today is that there is too much information on anything and everything. Think about health care. People are evaluating 10 million tests on all types of vitamins, chemicals and foods. Sometimes this particular food is good for you and now they prove it is bad for you. Looking at too much information confuses most of us.

The key to wisdom comes from good advisors and good experts. It is better to listen to a few people who know what they are doing than to listen to everything that comes on TV or Internet. And a good advisor can help you sort out the best investment options and the best investment plans, and help you find the best experts to listen to. A good financial advisor is like your human browser that helps you find the servers.

Good luck trying to sort through all the opinions on the economy, the stock market and how to measure a mutual fund. I don't know how most people are going to figure that out without making it a full-time job. A few may do it well as a hobby, and some may have a natural talent for it — but most people don't. It is also very time-consuming. I personally do not have the time in my profession to sit around on the Internet and randomly go through all types of stock charts, economic information and forecasts.

79

What will happen to Medicare and Social Security?

The federal budget situation, which I predicted in my 1992 book, is going to get better — and there will be more surpluses. More payroll taxes will go into Social Security and Medicare, and these systems will be financially stronger and have fewer cutbacks than anticipated. A problem pops up, however, as the economy turns down due to declines in spending by baby boomers in 2009 and later. Lower payroll taxes and lower tax revenues for government will exacerbate the downturn in the economy. It will deteriorate further as boomers get older and start to draw these benefits from the government. We still see a crisis long term. However the economy will be very strong during the next decade and people may demand a raise in their benefits because they feel the country can easily afford it.

80

What will be the effect of the Internet on our economy and our society?

The Internet is being touted today as a great entertainment medium. That's what kids are using it for. Fewer of us realize, however, that the Internet is the greatest direct marketing medium ever invented. It is capable of customization and fast response. As its video capabilities develop, it will be able to deliver the human touch in a way it can't right now. Then, physicians will be able to communicate with their patients and maintain relationships with them over the Internet. And they will be able to refer or bring in specialists on an Internet conference. I think the real Internet will show itself when more consumers learn to use it — and not just businesses.

When we get these capabilities that allow personalized service over the Internet, people would still come in to see a physician for a checkup or a financial advisor. But a lot of the relationship could be better managed over the Internet in a way that's more efficient both for the patient and the doctor. I think the Internet is going to be an incredible productivity driver for the economy. It is going to put all industries back in consumer's hands, which is why the medical professionals should ask him or herself, "How would the consumer design our industry?" rather than "How would the HMOs design it or the key producers design it?" The Internet is going to give consumers more power to deal with who they want, when they want and to get more information about the effectiveness of the product and service providers out there. It is going to be very efficient for the economy, very beneficial for consumers and will probably cause the biggest productivity explosion in our history.

81

How will the Internet help or hurt physicians?

It depends upon how physicians position themselves. If you use the Internet to increase personalization and add more value to your relationship to patients, it will help you. If you ignore the Internet and let someone else fill this vacuum with your patients, then it will hurt your practice. We see similar trends in other industries too. The health care industry is similar to real estate: they both involve important one-time events that people don't deal with day-to-day and rely on professional and personal advice to navigate successfully. Obviously, I do not see discount surgery on the Internet. I do not see the Internet hurting physicians.

82

What is your opinion of investors who deposit most if not all of their retirement money into index funds?

This strategy guarantees that you'll do as well as the market if you have the discipline to hold those investments. I never think investing in index funds is the best strategy because there are always sectors outperforming within our economy. Our economy favors sectors like health care, financial services, and technology over the next decade. I think investors would do better to concentrate on those sectors and use diversification to lower their risk. To put this index fund strategy in perspective, index funds have done very well from 1995 to 1998; but that's a short time period. Most good actively managed mutual funds for prior time periods and probably in the next decade will outperform index funds. I would not project the good short-term outperformance of index funds far into the future.

83

Do you recommend online investing for those of us who feel comfortable using the Internet?

If you are going to invest yourself, it is more efficient, faster and easier to get information from the Internet. I, as a general rule, do not recommend do-it-yourself investing anymore than I would recommend do-it-yourself surgery or do-it-yourself health care. Investing is getting more complex. And there are significant advantages for investors who combine everything from mortgages to credit strategies to estate planning and insurance by dealing with a primary financial advisor. This is not a simple field; it is not just as simple as finding the right mutual fund and buying it to build your retirement plan.

Anyone who values his or her time, or who has a lucrative profession, cannot afford to spend the amount of time required to do something someone else can do as well or better — even at a fee. They delegate things to experts.

That's how they have gotten richer over time. Not only can you make mistakes, but also it takes a lot of time. Would you rather spend the extra six to seven hours weekly with your family or traveling — or on the Internet watching stocks and tracking charts? I don't think online investing makes sense for most professionals, simply because they don't have the time —and time is the greatest scarcity of this era. In short, I don't think it pays off. The fact is, most studies have shown that most investors under perform and the more they trade, the more they under perform.

84

What can demographic trends tell investors?

I guess the better question is what can't demographic trends tell investors? I show in my books that we know when the average family eats and buys the most potato chips in their lifetimes; when their kids are in their calorie cycle around age 14 — the peak of calorie impact. With today's computer models, we can predict, down to zip code and neighborhood blocks, on age, income and lifestyle. We could predict the whole debt cycle of the 80s and early 90s just by watching baby boomers borrowing money to buy their first home — a predictable demographic cycle. And we could foresee that the inflation of the 70s, with the expense of raising young people and educating them, would all disappear with the baby bust of the 80s.

Now, as baby boomers have moved into their investment cycle, beginning in the mid-90s, we're seeing an incredible boom in the economy and an acceleration in stock prices While they continue to spend and earn money and be productive as workers, we've got a golden decade ahead of us —purely due to demographics. This golden decade has nothing to do with the federal deficit or government. I predicted in 1992 that the government deficit would disappear around 1998. This was because tax revenues increased as a result of a very strong economy and inflation rates continued to fall, easing the burden to finance the deficit. All of this was purely demographic.

Demographics drive social trends and technology trends. New generations spur technologies when they are young, and they bring revolutions in business that changes business practices and business models. I find that almost everything can be traced to simple demographic trends. The upside of this is it makes it easy for people who are not sophisticated economists to understand the economy. In fact, we can understand the economy better than the experts can.

85

What effect does legal or illegal immigration have on futurists who study demographic trends?

Immigrants come to our country; they work, live and buy products here. To predict demographic trends, we use a computer model to take the age data we have on immigrants. Then we adjust all legal immigrants into a birth index that predicts trends based on the ages that most people do things. We also estimate immigration in the future. You have to take immigration into account because these are real people adding to the trends, demographically.

86

What is the biggest mistake investors make?

I would say overconfidence. A huge ego trip goes with all the best-selling books and TV commercials. You know the one with a hippie who has a yacht behind his limousine, and kid who has a helicopter in his front yard. It's the get-rich-quick thing that's the biggest mistake. In contrast, great investors like Warren Buffett and Peter Lynch make money by systematically investing it and systematically beating the market. You don't do that by trading on whims and emotions. You don't do that by jumping on Internet stocks when they are hot and jumping out just before the top because nobody catches that. Or even buying the hottest mutual fund.

I think the best approach for investors is to do the following:
1. Be clear about your goals and your risk tolerance.
2. Develop a plan for systematic investing. That's why I think a good financial advisor can help keep you on that system. People say all the time that I am not going to sell when the market is down because I know it will come back. But when the market is down 20 percent, it looks like it is going to be down 40 percent.
3. Have a plan and stick to it. That's the way to prevent mistakes. People end up letting their emotions get in the way of logic when it comes to investing. We as human beings just don't seem to be wired to be good investors.

You can be a great doctor or a great lawyer and still be a poor investor. We all know who ended up buying the tax shelters of the 80s. It wasn't the average Joe; it was some of the brightest physicians, lawyers and business executives chasing another get-rich-quick scheme to save a bunch of taxes.

87

You mentioned that physicians should be looking at retirement differently. What do you mean?

We are going to live longer than the generation before us and we are going to want to be more active. I think retirement is a misnomer these days. I believe the new inflection point in our lives is the mid-life crisis. This is when our kids start to leave the nest, in the late 40s or early 50s for most people. This is the time to start redesigning your life. You have the freedom and no longer have the daily obligations of children, and you may have attained satisfaction within your career. Questions you may wish to ask yourself are: Do I want to start my own business? Do I want to start a nonprofit foundation? Do I want to work part time? Do I want to move to Aspen or Hilton Head or the Caribbean and start a practice there?

This is the time you may wish to reevaluate your life and decide if you want an active retirement in your 50s, when you have better health and more choices, or wait until your 70s when you stop working. You have the choice to build a satisfying profession or career, even if it is part-time or nonprofit, and sustain it well into your 70s or 80s. Part of my own retirement planning process is asking myself, "What do I have to do now with my financial investments so that I'll be able to afford a great second half of my life?"

88

What advice would you give physicians?

I would not take the short-term approach by looking at the developments of the last decade and project them forward. Everything goes in cycles. Every industry and every profession flourishes at times and then gets more competitive and consolidates more. For the past few years, we've been going through a consolidation type of phase in health care. Here's why the industry is moving into a flourishing phase:

1. Health care is something people use more as they age, and the baby boomers are going to be aging for the rest of their lives. This massive generation makes health care a good growth industry.
2. Health care is not as subject to the ups and downs of the economy as many other industries are, which makes it more stable.
3. The industry is also growing as a percentage of Gross Domestic Product (GDP). Food, oil, resources, and many major industries of the past are shrinking their percentage of GDP.
4. I think that the Internet and the expansion of new technologies for improving and extending life make the medical profession more lucrative. Physicians just have to position themselves properly to use these new technologies, to add value to their patients, and to get out of the HMO/discount mode. I think this will happen in the next 10 years. I would not discourage my children from pursuing a career in medicine or health care based solely on the trends of the last decade. That's just too short term. By the time they go to school and get all their degrees, we're bound to be in a different world.

89

Any opinions on investing in precious metals? Real estate?

For as long as I can remember, I have been telling people that precious metals aren't the place to be. Gold is losing its monetary value. The central banks are selling it. They are saying, "We don't need this stuff anymore." I like real estate selectively; real estate will do well in a good economy with low interest rates. However it is not going to be an outperformer except where the demographics show that demand will be high. This would be mostly in resort and vacation home real estate because baby boomers are now moving into these areas. There are a lot of areas in the stock market I prefer more than general commercial real estate.

90

You have recently created a mutual fund, The AIM Dent Demographic Trends Fund, which invests in companies likely to benefit from the demographic trends identified by your research. Are these all large cap companies? Are they only U.S. companies? In what sectors are you investing?

We aim to buy what I call "S Curve" companies; those that demonstrate very strong growth in revenues and earnings as they move from their introductory or innovation stage into mainstream market acceptance. This is shown by the following graph, "S Curve" Companies. About 60 percent of these companies are large cap, 20 to 30 percent small cap, and the rest international.

We are looking for companies with attractive growth potential.

We also look for sectors that will be most affected by baby boom spending in the next decade. They include technology, health care and financial services sectors. This fund is designed to outperform the S&P 500 without taking substantially higher risks.

91

What factors do you base the selection process for individual stocks?

We put the "S Curve" theory into practice by selecting individual stocks based on management, sales revenues, new product lines and most of all, company earnings.

92

Any comments on biotech trends?

Yes, I think that during the next decade, we start to see real biotech revolutions. The human and health care applications, which are starting to show promise, are still in their early stages. I search for sectors that look like they are going to be strong. I believe that small cap or small biotech companies fit this description now. I feel they are much like the computer companies of the late 70s on. We are going to see a lot of action in biotech, and its going to start to become more of a mainstream trend in the next decade; really, over the rest of our lifetime. I think that biotech is the real information revolution. It's much more complex and much more in depth human application come from understanding DNA structures than just using computers to automate office work. I think that biotech is going to be a huge trend over the long term.

It's probably going to start extending our lifespan at an accelerated rate —somewhere after about 2010 is my guess from looking at past cycles. I think it's going to start to show its stuff in the next decade. Everyone should take developments in biotech very seriously in the coming decade.

93

What is the Echo Baby Boom? What effect will it create?

It's the baby boom that followed the giant baby boom. It went from a low in births in 1975 to a peak into 1990. We may see another short birth cycle before it peaks out. These kids are up to elementary school and junior high school and high school right now; just starting to enter college. They are going to cause a whole wave of changes behind the baby boomers. They are entering the work force and entering college, so colleges are starting to expand again. They need more commercial real estate now.

The echo baby boomers are also trying new brand names in clothes. That's what new generations do — and ultimately they will move into apartments and get married during the early part of the 21st Century. After 2002, they will help accelerate spending on top of the baby boomers, because when people around ages 25 to 26 get married, they spend money at the fastest growth rate. This will bring even more vitality to our economy, particularly around 2002 to 2003.

94

When do you think investment opportunities will be favorable in Japan?

The demographics in Japan are against us until 2004. You could say the Japanese market is up 25 percent from their lows. Well, the Korean market has more than tripled; Hong Kong has more than doubled from its lows. Since the strength of demographics is in Korea, Hong Kong and Singapore, why not invest in those countries? Japan has made a poor showing compared to those countries. Even Indonesia has more than doubled from its lows. Japan is the laggard; so why invest in the laggard when the demographics are unfavorable? Even though the Japanese economy may trickle up, I think it will also trickle down at times. It just is not the best sector. That would be like buying oil stocks long term instead of technology, financial services or health care, which are more favored by demographics.

95

Any opinions on investing in foreign companies?

Demographics will tell you which areas of the world have more strength. Japan is still in a weak cycle, despite their little bounce recently with the comeback of Asia. Korea has incredible demographics; so does Hong Kong and Singapore. Prices will not keep those markets down for long.

If you want to buy foreign stocks, it's hard to keep track of it all. It's better to buy solid mutual or index funds or solid giant companies that you know. It's pretty hard to ferret out small cap companies to invest in Japan. It is hard enough to buy or find the right ones to invest in here. I think the international arena can be attractive in the next decade largely because the U.S. has given a wake-up call to the rest of the world by showing the direction in which things are going.

What we are doing is successful, and the rest of the world is going to follow. Demographics are very strong in most parts of the world except Japan. I think international is going to be a better sector for investors than in the past. You just have to find a way to invest in it that makes sense for you.

96

What will be the long-term effect of our trade imbalance?

There is not a big long-term effect. Just like consumers go through times in their lives when they borrow to build for the future and times when they harvest and save more, so do countries. Deficits are ways of importing more products to finance the cycle. Our dominance in key sectors going forward, such as technology, will give us trade surpluses down the line.

I do not take substantial account of trade surpluses and deficits in my long-term forecasts, because they don't make much of a difference. Instead, they tend to balance each other out. The same holds true for currencies.

We've had times when the yen was strong and then when the yen was weak. It's a symptom, not a cause, and not a real predictor of future growth. In a natural cycle, it's fine to have deficits and it's fine to have surpluses. It balances out over time.

97

Some economists are predicting the emergence of three dominant currencies; the dollar, the euro and the yen; and that individual nations will give up their currencies and adopt one of these three. What is your opinion of this prediction?

The dollar will still be the strongest. The three strong currencies are more of a check and balance system. I don't think this will change economics much or the trends we are forecasting. I think it is a good development. What you are really seeing is three major regional trading areas: Europe/Northern Africa, Asia, and North America/South America. Eventually these three trading areas will merge into one market.

98

You have documented well-known successful predictions. Do you have any prediction surprises that you care to share with us?

The biggest lesson I learned came from the biggest forecasting mistake I made was in the late 80s. Based on demographics, I predicted a two-year recession because of the drop in births during World War II. This drop in births would cause a dip in spending in most countries around the world. I predicted that Japan would go into a long downturn and that the U.S. would emerge from this stronger than ever.

The mistake I made was overestimating the impact of Japan's recession on the U.S. economy, and thinking it would cause a deflation wave that would make our recession much worse. It did not occur. What I learned from this experience was that the problems in Japan had very little impact in the U.S.

99

Do you recommend investing in bonds if I have more than a five-year time horizon?

No. Bonds have had a history of not returning as much as stocks, and that holds true for this boom too. Given that inflation has fallen so dramatically since 1980, bonds have been a very good investment, up to now given their risk. We don't see that in the next decade. We see that inflation is going to stay at relatively low flat rates and bonds are going to yield somewhere between four to six percent on 30-year U.S. government bonds. There is going to be little appreciation from disinflation, and bonds will be one of the lowest performing asset classes in the next decade.

We think conservative investors should move more toward high-income stocks. I would also recommend they buy multinational companies that are diversified around the world, that are well-established brand names, and that systematically draw income out of these stock portfolios. I am not recommending buying bonds as a general rule in the next decade. Bonds will be good in the decade after that, when our economy starts falling after 2009. I would recommend buying bonds then when bonds will do better than stocks.

100

Any comments specifically for physicians?

Yes. Reposition yourself to add more value and to help your patients make more and better choices, so that you don't have to be subject to these top-down HMO systems. The wealthy are getting wealthier and parts of our economy are doing very well. There are people who are willing to pay for someone who is competent, objective, can offer them choices and a superior level of service. I would get out of the treadmill and say, "I'm not going to be a slave to the HMO system" and figure the best way to do follow this strategy.

101

As a futurist, what advice would you give young people to help them prepare for the challenges of the 21st Century?

That's a tough one. There are some great fields to go into, like biology —it's the new science. It is the network world on the science side. Of course computer sciences and business. I think business education is good for anyone — regardless of his or her career. In general, I would say that you have to find what you really do best. Young people shouldn't say, "I have to be 100 percent sure of my career choice by age 21." These days, people are taking longer to mature, longer to experiment, and longer to find their optimal careers.

I think that most people are finding real career directions in their late rather than early 20s nowadays. So give yourself some space! If you are interested in health care or financial services, it's okay to have direction, but try not to buttonhole yourself too early in a specialty. The same holds true for marriage. I don't recommend running out and getting married early, as many people did in the past, at age 21 or 22. If you can wait until you are clearer about the direction of your life, the chances of your marriage working out successfully are much better.

Chapter 3
Understanding Stocks and Bonds

More investors seem to realize that equities offer the best protection in the long run against inflation, but recognize that they are also the greatest threat to their portfolio in the short run. Bonds are supposed to be less risky than stocks, but many bond investors were shocked to see their account values plummet as the Federal Reserve raised short-term interest rates six times within one year.

In 1999, NASDAQ investors were generously rewarded as the NASDAQ rose 86 percent. Some frustrated bond holders and bond fund investors grew impatient in January and February 2000, as the value of their holdings continued to decline. They switched to tech/Internet stocks and funds to make up for their fixed-income losses. In March and April 2000, the NASDAQ dropped 37 percent from its highs.

Numerous convincing studies have concluded that proper asset allocation is responsible for more than 90 percent of the return for individual portfolios — as expressed by Dr. Richard Marston in his earlier interview following Chapter I. Asset allocation is the process of determining which class of assets to invest in.

I receive many questions from physicians (mostly by email) about investing in two sectors: health care and technology. Following this chapter are interviews with two experts in these fields: Lloyd Kurtz and Andrew Barrett.

102

What is the "cockroach theory?"

It's a theory regarding disappointing news found in forecasts or statements made by public corporations. And it goes like this: Cockroach sightings and bad news are rarely isolated events. If you see *one* cockroach there are probably dozens more hiding nearby. The same goes for bad news.

103

My bank trust department needed a "CUSIP number" for a misplaced municipal bond certificate. What is a CUSIP number?

It is a unique nine-character identification number used to identify individual securities. It functions just like a fingerprint, so it is also used to facilitate identifying lost or misplaced bonds. The term is based on the work of the Committee on Uniform Securities Identification Procedures.

104

I know that the Wilshire 5000 is the broadest stock index, but which stocks does it consist of?

The Wilshire 5000 Equity Index (despite what its name suggests) includes approximately 7,600 American stocks (including NYSE and AMEX stocks and the most active over-the-counter ones). For everything you wanted to know about this index plus more, visit their website www.wilshire.com.

105

When are trading halts triggered to suspend trading on the stock exchange?

New York Stock Exchange (NYSE) Rule 80B spells out how trading halts are calculated and when they are activated. Trading halts are figured at the beginning of each quarter in terms of Dow 30 declines in one trading day of 10 percent (Level 1), 20 percent (Level 2) and 30 percent (Level 3).

Trading is halted on the NYSE when:
A "Level 1" Halt is declared when there is a 10 percent decline:
1) before 2:00 p.m. eastern time (trading halts for 1 hour)
2) at 2:00 p.m. or later before 2:30 p.m. (trading halts for 30 minutes)
3) at 2:30 p.m. or later (trading continues unless a "Level 2" Halt occurs)

A "Level 2" Halt is declared when there is a 20 percent decline:
1) before 1:00 p.m. (trading halts for 2 hours)
2) at 2:00 p.m. or later (trading does not resume for rest of day)

A "Level 3" Halt is declared when there is a 30 percent decline:
        At any time (trading is halted and does not resume for rest of the day)

Beginning April 1, 2000 halts are triggered when the Dow 30 declines on the previous day by:
        Level 1: .... 1,050 points
        Level 2: .... 1,530 points
        Level 3: .... 2,000 points

106

Why would a company do a reverse-split with their shares?

A reverse-split raises the stock price by reducing the number of outstanding shares; a regular split lowers the stock price by increasing the number of outstanding shares. Let's look at an example. When a $100 stock splits 4-for-1, each stockholder's number of shares are quadrupled and the new price per share becomes $25. Stock splits make owning shares more affordable and therefore more attractive to investors. So why would a company do a reverse-split and make them more expensive? Let's look at another example. Stocks that sell for less than $5 a share (called penny stocks) are considered speculative, high-risk investments. A reverse-split may be done to increase the price per share of the stock and enhance the company's image. (Especially important when a merger or acquisition is in the works.) Also, some stock exchanges have minimum price requirements for listing stocks or maintaining listings. Companies whose stocks are heading for the minimum listable price may initiate a reverse-split.

107

What is the New York Stock Exchange Advance-Decline Line? How is it calculated?

The New York Stock Exchange's advance-decline line ("AD line") is calculated daily by subtracting the number of stocks that have dropped in price that day from those that have risen. Stocks whose price remains unchanged for the day are omitted. The AD line is a much broader market indicator than the Dow Jones Industrial Average, which consists of only 30 large cap companies.

108

I saw the term "reverse takeover" in the Wall Street Journal. What does it mean?

A reverse takeover happens when a corporation takes over another corporation and assumes the identity of the firm that has been acquired. Acquiring companies change their names to the acquired company to enhance their images or assume better-known identities. Examples of reverse takeovers include Profitt's takeover of Saks Fifth Avenue, Primerica's takeover of Travelers, and NationsBank's takeover of Bank America.

109

I'm a 33-year-old single physician employed by the Veterans Administration. For the past four years, I've been withholding the maximum I'm allowed for retirement — $2,000 a year — to my IRA. Right now, it's worth is about $11,000. I'm invested in the Vanguard Index Fund and have diversified with international securities and bonds. I also keep six months worth of expenses in a money market fund for emergencies. Does it make sense to keep my entire equity portfolio in an investment that tracks the Wilshire 5000 (since it covers everything in the stock market) and not worry about small cap or value stocks?

Congratulations! You're on the right track to become financially independent. I commend your self-discipline for saving and investing.

First, a comment about your IRA. If you convert your IRA to a Roth IRA (as long as your adjusted gross income will be less than $100,000), you'll have to pay roughly an additional

$3,000 in taxes. However, the growth of your new Roth IRA will be tax-deferred and will not be subject to taxes when you start taking distributions in 40+ years. Let's assume you make no more contributions to your IRA and it grows 12 percent annually. The $11,000 will double every six years; at age 69 your original $8,000 investment will have grown to more than $700,000 tax-free.

Now about your equity portfolio. Since your investment time horizon is more than 20 years, convert the bond portion of your portfolio into equity. You're not quite right about the Wilshire 5000 covering "everything" in the stock market. It's true that it includes all NYSE and AMEX stocks and the most active over-the-counter stocks, but it does not include equities outside of the U.S.

110

What are crossover refunded municipal bonds?

These are revenue bonds with a provision that they be refunded early when certain debt service requirements are met. Crossover refunded municipal bonds are used for financing toll roads, toll bridges and electric utilities. If you buy these types of tax-free bonds, realize that they may be pre-refunded before the stated maturity date.

111

I was surprised to learn that I have to pay alternative minimum tax (AMT) on income from some of my tax-free bonds. Aren't tax-free bonds supposed to be tax-free?

Interest earned on certain types of tax-free or municipal bonds is subject to the AMT both for those that are held individually or those held in bond funds. Tax-exempt interest on private activity municipal bonds is an AMT preference item that generated an additional AMT liability on your tax return. When buying municipal bonds, ask your broker "are they subject to AMT?" Normally you will get a slightly higher yield from AMT bonds.

Congress created AMT so that "taxpayers with substantial income would pay their fair share of taxes." It would also impose a tax that would ignore losses from tax shelters, accelerated depreciation and drilling costs and is currently calculated with your regular tax. You figure your regular tax and then your AMT tax; whichever is larger is what you pay. For AMT calculations, certain income items called AMT preference items and adjustments, previously excluded from calculating your adjusted gross income (AGI) such as your tax-free income from private muni bonds, are added back before recalculating AGI.

Congress failed to index this tax for inflation and many investors may now painfully find themselves subject to AMT taxes. As stated in the April 28, 1999, Wall Street Journal, "If Congress does nothing, more than nine million returns will be hit by this tax in 2009, up from 823,000 in 1999."

112

What is meant by the "Ice Cream Effect" on tech stocks?

The "Ice Cream Effect" is a euphemism for the seasonal slowdown in order activity that often occurs during summer months, which generally result in weaker third quarter earnings and lower stock prices for tech companies. Conversely, holiday-related orders tend to stimulate buying in November and December, which often drives up expected earnings and stock prices. This buoyant influence is known as the "Santa Clause Effect."

113

What are Eurobonds?

Eurobonds are international bonds sold outside of the country in whose currency they are issued. For example, Eurodollar bonds are dollar-denominated bonds sold anywhere outside the U.S., including areas other than in Europe. Eurosterling bonds and Euroyen bonds are examples of Eurobonds. Eurosterling bonds are sold outside the U.K. and are denominated in British currency and Euroyen bonds are sold outside of Japan and are denominated in yen. There is one other type of international bond, the foreign bond. Foreign bonds are issued in the currency of the country in which they are sold. An example of a foreign bond would be French corporation's bond that is dollar denominated in the U.S.

114

Why has the value of my preferred stocks dropped so much lately?

There are two reasons. First, the recent increase in interest rates. The 30-year U.S. Treasury bond (or "long bond") has steadily moved up. As fixed income rates (bond coupons and preferred dividends) go up, their market value drops. Second, there's been an increase in supply due to unusually high issuance in the syndicate market. An increase in supply (all things being constant) causes price decreases.

115

I am seven years away from retirement and have $462,000 invested in my deferred compensation plan. Several months ago I transferred everything from stocks to money markets because I felt the stock market was getting ready to correct itself. What do you think of this tactic?

This tactic or strategy is called "timing the market." If you want to be a market timer, you have to be correct twice: once when you decide to sell and go into cash; and once when you decide to get out of cash and reenter the market. Otherwise you are selling low and buying high. I don't recommend this as an effective way to managing your investment portfolio — because I have never met anyone who is a good market timer. In 1998, the Standard & Poor's 500 (an index of 500 major U.S. corporation stocks) increased approximately 28 percent. If an investor were out of the market during the five best performing days of the market in 1998, his or her return was only one percent. It's time in the market that counts, not timing the market. No one can predict how the market will perform on a daily basis.

116

My 27-year-old son is considering quitting his job with a major corporation and becoming a full-time day trader. Although he's had success trading his own account since he started doing it last year, I'm concerned that he may be making a mistake. What do you recommend?

Day trading is very exciting. So is gambling in a casino — when you're winning. The October, 1999, issue of Worth Magazine has an article on day trading called "Day Dreaming." It cites statistics from the North American Securities Administrators Association (NASAA) showing that only 11.5 percent of day traders are profitable. The article continues to say that "Seventy percent of day traders are so bad that they are likely not just to lose money but to lose all of their money." I think you are justified in being concerned; your son is considering entering a business where the likelihood of failure is 88.5 percent. Would you have become a physician if you faced these odds of failure? Probably not.

117

I own SPDR shares (traded on the American Stock Exchange) and an S&P 500 index fund. Is there a need to have more than one fund which tracks the same index?

No. There's no need to duplicate your investments. SPDR stand for Standard & Poor's Depository Receipts that represent ownership in the S&P 500 Trust. This is a long-term unit investment trust. It has been established to accumulate and hold a portfolio of common stocks whose goal is to track the price performance and dividend yield of the S&P 500 Composite Stock Price Index. SPDRs are traded on the American Stock Exchange and trade for 1/10 the value of the S&P 500 Index. Diamonds are similar to SPDRs. They represent ownership in a unit trust holding a portfolio of the 30 stocks of the Dow Jones Industrial Averages(DJIA). Diamonds trade for 1/100 the value of the DJIA.

118

Recently the Dow 30 dropped four companies and replaced them with four others. Does this have any significance? What are the 30 companies that make up this average?

The editors of The Wall Street Journal select the companies that make up the Dow 30. Dow Jones & Company publishes the Journal. The four companies dropped were Union Carbide (UK), Sears (S), Goodyear Tire & Rubber (GT) and Chevron (CHV). The four companies added were Home Depot (HD), Intel (INTC) Microsoft (MSFT) and SBC Communications (SBC).

Since the Dow Jones Industrial Average (DJIA) was created

in 1896, all component companies have always been listed on the New York Stock Exchange (NYSE). This is the first exception: Intel and Microsoft are listed on the NASDAQ (National Association of Securities Dealers Automated Quotations System) and not the NYSE. Paul E. Steuger, managing editor of the Journal, said, "The changes we are announcing October 26, 1999, will make the DJIA even more representative of the evolving U.S. economy, as the Average — and the nation — enter a new century."

Observers held that the four additions would jump-start or supercharge the DJIA because the past five-year overall growth rate for the four new companies exceeded 500 percent; whereas the growth rate in the same period for the four companies dropped was 59 percent. Let's examine these eight companies from two different perspectives; dividend yields and price earnings ratios (P/E).

Companies Deleted P/E Dividend Yield	Companies Added
Chevron .... 56 .... 2.9%	Intel .... 38 ... 0.2%
Sears .... 9 .... 3.2%	Microsoft .... 60 ...... 0%
Goodyear .... 19 .... 3.3%	SBC Communications ... 31 ... 1.9%
Union Carbide .... 29 .... 1.5%	Home Depot .... 61 ... 0.2%
Average .... 26 .... 2.7%	*Average* .... 48 ... 0.6%

The P/E of the four new companies is almost double the companies they replaced whereas the new dividend yield is not even 1/4 that of the old companies. Obviously, investors prefer capital appreciation or growth to income, especially when tax policies encourage this strategy. The maximum long-term capital gains rate is 20 percent versus the maximum ordinary income tax rate of 39.6 percent. For additional information, please visit the Dow Jones website: www.dowjones.com. As of November 15, 1999, the Dow 30 consists of the following companies (stock symbols are in parentheses):

Allied Signal (ALD)	International Bus Mach. (IBM)
Aluminum Co. of America (AA)	International Paper (IP)
American Express (AXP)	J.P. Morgan (JPM)
AT&T (T)	Johnson & Johnson (JNJ)
Boeing (B)	McDonald's (MCD)
Caterpillar (CAT)	Merck (MRK)
Citigroup (C)	Microsoft (MSFT)
Coca-Cola (KO)	Minn. Mining & Manuf. (MMM)
DuPont (DD)	Philip Morris (MO)
Eastman Kodak (EK)	Proctor & Gamble (PG)
Exxon (XON)	SBC Communications (SBC)
General Electric (GE)	United Technologies (UTX)
General Motors (GM)	Wal-Mart Stores (WMT)
Hewlett-Packard (HWP)	Walt Disney (DIS)
Home Depot (HD)	
Intel (INTC)	

119

What is the significance of duration when buying a bond?

Duration is the average time for a bond's interest and principal payments to be repaid. Investors can reduce their exposure to interest rate risk by buying bonds with shorter durations.

120

I am a 69-year-old retired internist in the 36 percent tax bracket. Is there a formula for me to compare a tax-free and taxable investment?

Yes, you need to select the investment providing the greater net after tax return. The formula for calculating the taxable equivalent return = tax-free yield divided by one — your tax bracket. You are considering buying a taxable bond with an 8.5 percent coupon or a tax-free bond with a six percent coupon and you are in the 36 percent tax bracket. By using the above tax equivalent return formula, .06 divided by .64 (we get .64 by 1.00 - .36). The answer or quotient is .0938 or 9.38 percent is the tax equivalent yield or return for a six percent tax-free bond, which is a better return than an eight percent taxable bond. You can also calculate the after tax return from the taxable investment, .085 X .64 = .0544 or 5.44 percent is less return than the six percent tax-free investment.

121

Why does the Federal Reserve raise interest rates when it causes the stock market to drop?

The primary objective of the Federal Reserve is not to keep stock prices high. As the US central bank, the Fed tries to pursue a policy of maintaining stability in our economy; stable growth, stable prices and full employment. They do this by regulating the supply of credit and money (monetary policy).

When the Fed thinks prices are rising too fast (inflation) and wants to slow the economy, it raises interest rates to make borrowing more costly. This normally discourages consumers and businesses from spending, reduces economic activity and lessens demand for goods and services. As demand drops, the supply increases. With increased supply, firms are less willing to raise prices and may have to cut prices, which causes a decline in their profits or earnings. When interest rates increase, bonds may become a more attractive investment alternative. This causes the intrinsic value of stocks to decline. Since the long-term value of a stock is based upon its earnings, increased borrowing costs make the company's breakeven point harder to attain and earnings drop.

122

Do you think the NASDAQ index will surpass the Dow Jones Industrial Average (DJIA)?

Probably not in the near future. Until recently, these two indices were distinctly different with no overlap of holdings. With the addition of Intel and Microsoft (two NASDAQ companies) to the Dow 30 or DJIA, I believe we'll see more NASDAQ companies added, possibly companies like CISCO and WCOM. As the overlap increases, the distinction between the two indices will lessen and the growth of the DOW 30 will be supercharged by the addition of these NASDAQ powerhouses.

123

Why are inflation indexed bonds yielding above four percent plus inflation? Historically, interest rates average three percent above inflation and don't carry a guarantee. They seem awfully good for the conservative investor. What's the catch?

Normally these investments trade three percent over the inflation rate for the life of the issue. It pays a semiannual coupon; you do not receive the inflation factor income until maturity or sale. However, in a taxable account (non-IRA) you receive a 1099 for phantom income and must pay taxes even though you never received the money. In my opinion, this investment does not keep up with your real cost of living. For example, prescription drug prices, fuel, tuition, nursing home costs are increasing much faster than the CPI.

124

What is a PEG ratio? How is it computed? What significance does it have?

The PEG ratio is two ratios divided by each other; the price/earnings multiple (PE) divided by the growth rate (G). The higher the PEG ratio, the more expensive the sector or the company.

125

How do I find a list of the upcoming IPOs before they're offered?

You can find a list of upcoming initial public offerings (IPOs) by going to www.ipo.com or checking the Monday edition of the Wall Street Journal, Section C.

126

Why have consumer cyclical stocks been some of the poorest performers this year?

The Federal Reserve has been trying to reduce inflationary pressures by raising interest rates to discourage consumers from spending. These interest rate hikes have depressed the market prices of consumer cyclical companies.

127

What is a tracking stock?

A tracking stock or targeted stock enables a parent company to issue a particular or distinctive security for a division/subsidiary without spinning off this company. A parent company may be in a sector that trades at 12 times earnings while the subsidiary may be in a much faster growing sector trading at 30 times earnings. By issuing a tracking stock for the faster growing subsidiary, the market price of the new issue or tracking stock will probably sell for 2-1/2 times the multiple of the parent company's market price. Tracking stockholders have claims on all the parent company's assets.

128

How can I check whether the NASD has disciplined my stockbroker?

You can call the NASD toll free hotline at 800-289-9999 or visit their website at www.nasdr.com and check out your broker. More agencies are providing consumers with information about licensed professionals. Patientwatch of Roslyn Heights, New York, offers consumers information on physicians by examining their education, specialized training and malpractice records. Their website is www.patientwatch.com.

129

My local broker receives a fee of a 1/4 percent per annum from the "family" of mutual funds in his "custody" for me. This excludes any activity on his part. Is this true? And, if this is so, can I have this non-activity fee returned to me if I maintain custodianship by working directly with the parent fund?

No. Think of this fee or "trail" as a built-in cost — the same way an airline ticket has a built-in fee if you use a travel agent to book your flight. There is no discount if you deal directly with the airline or buy your ticket from a travel agent. The same applies to a mutual fund company. It will not pay or discount this broker's fee if you deal directly.

130

Is there any difference between a financial planner and a certified financial planner?

According to Jane Bryant Quinn in her *Newsweek* column of September 13, 1999, "Anyone can pass out a business card that says financial planner, financial advisor or retirement specialist. You want the card to say CFP, meaning Certified Financial Planner. CFP licensees have passed a rigorous course that covers all aspects of personal finance. They are also required to keep their education up to date."

Interview with Lloyd Kurtz on Health Care

Lloyd Kurtz, a Chartered Financial Analyst (CFA), specializes in researching U.S. pharmaceutical, managed care, and biotechnology companies and industries. He is an Analyst and Director of Quantitative Research at Harris, Bretall Sullivan & Smith; a major money management firm based in San Francisco. Harris Bretall specializes in high growth companies for the long-term investor. Kurtz is a frequent and well-known speaker on healthcare topics, and our interview will focus on investing in health care. He can be reached at 800-388-4277 or lloydk@hbss.com.

131

As growth investors, what market sectors do you see having the best long-term growth prospects, aside from the technology and telecommunications sectors?

When we answer that question, we start with the real economy, not the stock market, because we believe that stock prices follow earnings. Industries with above-average earnings growth should achieve superior stock price performance over time. Setting aside technology and telecommunication, the other sectors that have consistently grown faster than the real economy over the past 20 years have been health care, consumer and finance.

132

What do you mean by the consumer sector?

Consumer discretionary spending, such as retail stores and restaurants, as opposed to things like energy and defense. We expect these trends to continue over the next few years.

133

What are the forces driving these sectors?

Demographics and healthy economy. The financial sector exploded as responsible monetary policy improved returns on financial assets. Then add the demographic wave of baby boomers investing in the stock market over the past two decades. The boomers are transforming the stock market just as they did the real estate market in the 1970s and universities and colleges in the 1960s. Deregulation has also played an important role.

We believe that baby boomer population will also be the most important force driving health care. It's important to understand how large this impact is going to be. The Bureau of the Census currently estimates that the number of people 55 and over in the U.S. will increase by 30 percent over the next 10 years, about three times faster than the overall population. Another way to look at it is to notice that 1933 was the trough year for births in the U.S. in this century — that means that the number of 65 year-olds troughed in 1998, and now will rise steadily for decades.

No matter how you analyze it, the U.S. health care system is going to have a massive increase in the volume of medical procedures that will need to be done and the volume of prescriptions that will be written.

134

Why do you feel health care will be attractive when managed care problems have disillusioned so many patients and physicians?

I think that managed care as we have known it is on the way out. In its old incarnation (particularly the early nineties version) managed care was all about controlling costs. The central premise was that health care was too expensive. The Clinton health care plan was largely motivated by a concern that the U.S. would not be able to afford all the health care it wanted. The Clinton policymakers reasoned that we might as well get onto a health care rationing system quickly and figure out how we were going to distribute those scarce resources.

Today, the political environment has been colored by the fact that the nation is being better run today than it was before, and that it is economically healthier. When you look at the proposals that have the greatest political support, they are not about cutting back, but about adding services like a prescription drug benefit. They also include proposals to cover the uninsured. So instead of taking health care services away from people who are currently getting them and giving them to the uninsured, now we're talking about delivering quality health care services to everyone. We know that that would be expensive, but it looks like we can afford it.

Meanwhile, people have become increasingly hostile towards managed care — and that has opened the doors for doctors to make more decisions. That is a relatively recent phenomenon. In late 1999, United Health Group (UNH) announced that they would no longer review doctor decisions on individual treatments. And no politician now thinks he or she can build a political campaign by talking about what a great thing managed care is.

The bottom line is that we now have a country that is intent on spending more money on health care. It is pretty clear at this stage of the game that we are not going to change over to a Canadian or British-style health care system that comes with tough rationing.

135

Any comments on U.S. health care delivery systems?

When a country puts together a health care system, it has a choice. It can have a standardized, centralized system, which is attractive because it can be very cheap. A lot of countries, the UK and Canada, for example, have centralized systems that are pretty rigidly run and tightly controlled from a cost perspective. But there is considerable pressure in those countries to move toward better benefits and less central control.

The U.S. represents the opposite extreme. We have very decentralized health care. Doctors make decisions as individual professionals; there is "medical czar" who tells doctors exactly how they must practice medicine. The benefit is that patients have a lot of choices, and they can identify a doctor whom they think is going to do the best job for them. This fosters innovation, and is one reason why so many important medical innovations come out of the U.S. But the downside of a decentralized system like ours is that it is expensive.

136

How large is the healthcare pie? What percentage of the U.S. Gross Domestic Product (GDP) is spent on health care?

The U.S. spends approximately 14 percent of its GDP on health care. Given what we have seen happen politically over the past few years and given the history of the baby-boomers, who don't like to settle for second-best, we expect that, rather than seeing that go down to a lower number like the 10 percent for Germany or six percent for UK, before the baby-boom generation is done, health care could be 20-25 percent of GDP.

As a Percentage of GDP

	Healthcare		*Healthcare*
U.S.	14.0%	Netherlands	8.5%
Germany	10.4%	Italy	7.6%
France	9.9%	Japan	7.3%
Canada	9.3%	U.K.	6.7%

Source: OECD Health Data, 1999

137

How has per-capita health care spending grown in relation to GDP growth?

Over the long term, per-capita health care spending has been ahead of GDP growth. The U.S. has consistently pursued a health care policy of making it a larger and larger portion of the GDP. Wherever the world is going, the U.S. will get there first, because we are an affluent, growing country, and what we decide to do with our disposable income will be something that influences other countries.

138

Do you think the pie can continue to grow?

I think so. This is counterintuitive for some people. Certainly there are a lot of people who believe the health care pie should be smaller, that there is enough money being spent on health care, and that the only question is how to divide it up and use it more efficiently.

But, when I look at the behavior of consumers, I get a different answer. I see the popularity of herbal remedies, chiropractors, and aromatherapy — many of these products address quality-of-life issues, rather than just health problems as they've traditionally been defined. The drug companies are also seeing that, because they are becoming more consumer-focused. Merck (MRK) with its Propecia drug for baldness and Pfizer (PFE) with Viagra are realizing that even if the health insurance companies won't pay for these drugs — the consumer will. Because of the strength of the consumer, we are going to see the health care pie increasing regardless of the decisions made at the governmental or insurance company level.

139

Does plastic surgery for cosmetic reasons fall into this category?

Yes. We will see more of that as the baby boomers continue to age.

140

How will the health care pie be divided?

The lion's share will go to the innovators. Now that hasn't always been true — in the 1960s and 1970s, it was hospitals and large medical institutions that got disproportionate shares of health care dollars. In the 1980s, practitioners got the larger share as shown by the following graph.

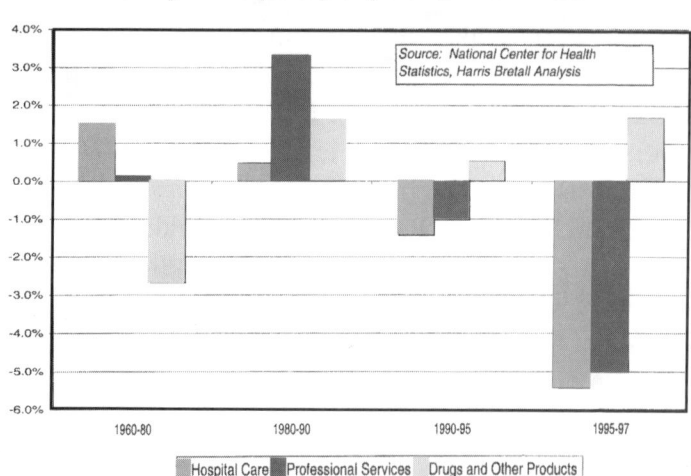

Change in Real per Capita Spending, vs. GDP Trend

Source: National Center for Health Statistics, Harris Bretall Analysis

Hospital Care | Professional Services | Drugs and Other Products

Now, the 1990s haven't been that great for any particular health care sector. But, clearly, the group that has done the best have been the large pharmaceutical makers. We expect that to continue. The reason is that drugs are a very cost-effective way to treat patients. If outcomes are reasonably close, payors usually find it more attractive to pay for a pill than for a labor-intensive therapy.

For example, in psychiatry, prescribing antidepressants has moved significant market share away from psychiatrists and toward drug companies. We'll see more of that as new drugs are developed.

141

Will the upcoming changes in healthcare create intergenerational conflicts?

It absolutely will. The problem is that many sick Americans are going to want expensive treatments. The American taxpayers will be asked to foot the bill and these taxpayers will be younger than those receiving the benefits. But I don't think there is much doubt about who is going to win this political battle. Older people have more political clout than anyone else – they come out in the rain to vote. When they are also as numerous as the baby boomer generation, my guess is that they will be setting the political tone for many years to come.

142

Which companies do you think will benefit from these demographic trends and which markets will be most affected?

You might expect, with an aging population, that you should buy nursing home stocks. But that benefit is still many years away for the nursing homes. The first boomers were born in 1946, so they are just now in their mid-50s. They need care from doctors more often than they did before, but they are not yet ready for nursing homes. Nursing home stocks won't benefit from the demographic wave for another 20 years or more.

We believe the companies that will do the best will be ones that have treatments for diseases that are peculiar to the stage of life that the boomers are at. For example, adult onset diabetes. One reason we have liked Bristol-Myers (BMY) is that they have a strong diabetes franchise. We like Pfizer in part because they will be introducing an inhaled insulin product that appears to have billion dollar potential.

Asthma should also be an important area. We have been positive on Genentech (DNA), which has reported positive results for a new monoclonal antibody for treatment of asthma — a completely new treatment approach that would be a very exciting opportunity should that drug receive approval. We also own Schering-Plough (SGP), which has a significant allergy/asthma franchise and a monoclonal of its own in development. Those are the kinds of companies we believe will have the best results over the next few years.

143

What is your investment philosophy in selecting stocks or companies?

We try to keep it simple. We focus on earnings growth. We're growth investors, but we don't always agree with the academic definitions of our discipline. Some academics say that a growth investor is someone who buys stocks with high-priced book ratios or high P/E ratios or buys stocks that happen to be going up. Our focus is on stocks with earnings that we believe will rise significantly over time. We believe that if we can identify these stocks and hold them for long periods, our clients will do well. That has been our philosophy for the last 25 years.

144

Would you say you are a bottom-up versus a top-down stock picker?

We do intense bottom-up analysis — but it happens within a top-down structure that focuses on what our aggregate risk profile should look like. But every company we buy for our clients has to stand on its own merits. It has to be a company that we believe has the ability to deliver earnings that grow over the long term or it won't get into our portfolio.

145

What is the difference between a bottom-up and top-down stock selector?

Stereotypically, a bottom-up person sits in a room and looks at one stock at a time, trying to identify stocks that are going to go up. A top-down person starts with the aggregate macroeconomic outlook and says, "I believe the economy will be strong next year. What kinds of stocks are going to prosper in that economic framework?" In the end, all investors have to do some of both. You cannot analyze a steel company without forming some expectation of the economic outlook for next year. If you are expecting a recession, chances are no matter how great that steel company is, it is not going to perform well during a recession.

So you have to have an economic framework. This is particularly important for the medical sector, because medical stocks are viewed as defensive names. If there is a significant economic slowdown, they have historically done well relative to the rest of the market, because they have pretty predictable earnings. When the economy accelerates, they often underperform the market.

We saw a very good example of that in 1998 and 1999. In 1998, the Standard and Poor's 500 operating earnings were roughly flat with 1997. And during that period, the S&P 500 materially underperformed the major drug stocks. In 1999, that situation reversed itself. Operating earnings for the S&P were up 14 percent over 1998, about the same as the average big drug company. So money migrated out of the drug stocks and back to the lower-P/E S&P 500. As a result, the S&P 500 outperformed the large drug stocks in 1999.

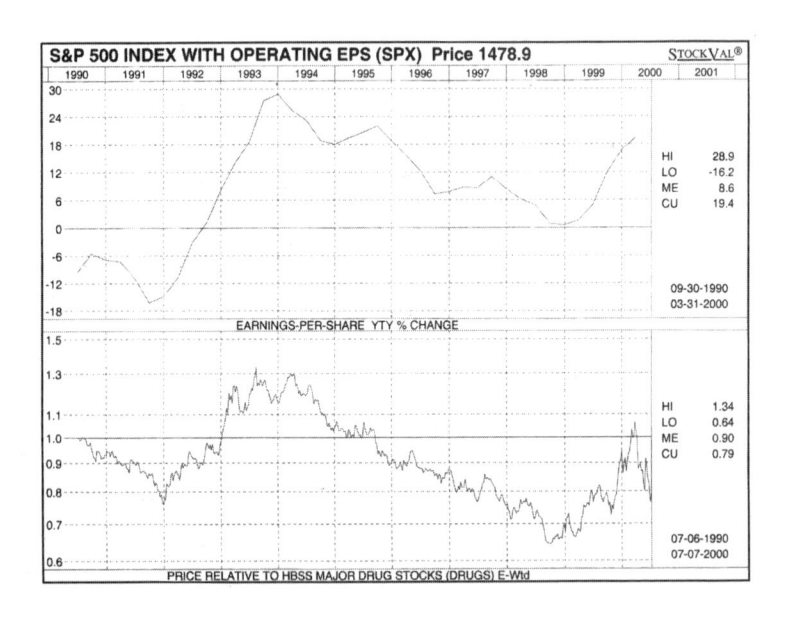

146

What percentage of health care is paid directly by the consumer? By third party payers? By government?

Today, consumers are spending less than they ever have on out-of-pocket health care expenditures. If you go back to the 1940s, most health care was paid for by the consumer at the time of service or shortly thereafter. As we got into the 1950s and 1960s, large corporations realized that it was very attractive to offer health care benefits to attract top-quality employees. And so by 1960, about 30 percent of health care bills were being reimbursed in some way. By 1980, that was up to about 70 percent. Today it's more like 80 percent. So when a patient sees a doctor, his or her out-of-pocket cost is only running about 20 percent of the total bill. The rest is paid by some other organization.

I suppose if you went back to 1940 and told people that in the year 2000 the government or large corporations would pay for 80 percent of your health care cost, their reaction would be: "That's a pretty good deal! That sounds terrific!"

But . . . when you delegate payments to someone else, you give up control. This loss of control is probably the main reason for the backlash we've seen against managed care, because some HMOs abused their patient responsibilities. And the patients said, "Hold it. You can't cut me off from treatments that I need and interfere with the medical judgment of my doctor." But when you let someone else pay 80 percent of your bills, you are probably giving them at least 80 percent of the influence over how these decisions will be made. It is sobering to consider that the rise of managed care reduced the voices of the two most important people— the doctor and the patient.

So, we are going to go reverse this trend over the next few

years because doctors and patients simply found this to be an unsatisfactory situation. But patients will have to pay more out-of-pocket as a result.

147

The large drug companies experienced depressed stock prices in 1993-94, but rebounded strongly after the Clinton health plan scare. Was this a blessing in disguise to toughen the survival instincts of these firms?

I think this was a blessing in disguise — for some companies. But there are some companies that still don't get it.

There are a couple of key points to take away from the Clinton health care episode. The first, which probably everyone in the industry learned, is that pharmaceutical companies are always politically vulnerable. They have expensive products that affect life-and-death issues. So, there is no way for them to disengage from the political process. Before the Clinton health care debate, there were people in the industry who thought that they could coast along relatively unobserved and not have to defend their business practices. Now, I think that this illusion has been permanently wiped away and the health care companies are among the most active lobbyists on health care issues in Washington. In recent years they have spent more money on lobbying than the health insurance industry and considerably more than the AMA.

But if all the companies learned the first lesson, I would guess that only about half learned the second, which was that, over the long term, they are not going to be allowed to grow profits just by raising prices. You must innovate. And the companies that took that lesson to heart and have really tried to implement it organizationally have done very well.

I am thinking, for example, of Pfizer, which markedly accelerated its research and development spending and, as a result, developed a very strong portfolio of young, outstanding growth products. The result was that it was one of the best-performing large drug stocks in the second half of the 1990s. At the same time, you have other companies that probably decided to stay with the old model, and try to raise prices in their existing pharmaceuticals and maybe cut research and development costs to show better short-term earnings. Some of these companies have already been merged out of existence, and more will disappear in the next few years.

148

How will the Internet impact health care?

It's already impacting it in a pretty significant way — I think doctors know this better than anyone. Patients are going to the Internet for health care advice and taking printouts to their doctors and saying, "I notice that I have this kind of asthma. I read on the Internet that with this kind of asthma, there's this new drug. Should I try it?"

This creates significant challenges for doctors. Number one, they have to deal with a lot of misinformation. Number two, they have to be as current as they possibly can be with the latest treatments. Patients are going to know about these procedures sooner than they did in the past and the pharmaceutical companies are getting very sophisticated about target marketing. As a result, new drugs are hitting peak earnings faster than they used to. In the old days, it might take a drug seven to 10 years to reach peak earnings, and today I suspect that that will be shortened to one to two years because of the improved efficiency and speed of disseminating health care information to the patients.

149

What will happen to HMOs? Are HMO stocks a good long-term investment?

No, we don't believe they are. When we look at the HMO stocks, we see a group of companies that for years were able to grow earnings simply by enrolling new members. The problem they have now is that it most of the people who are going to be in managed care have already enrolled.

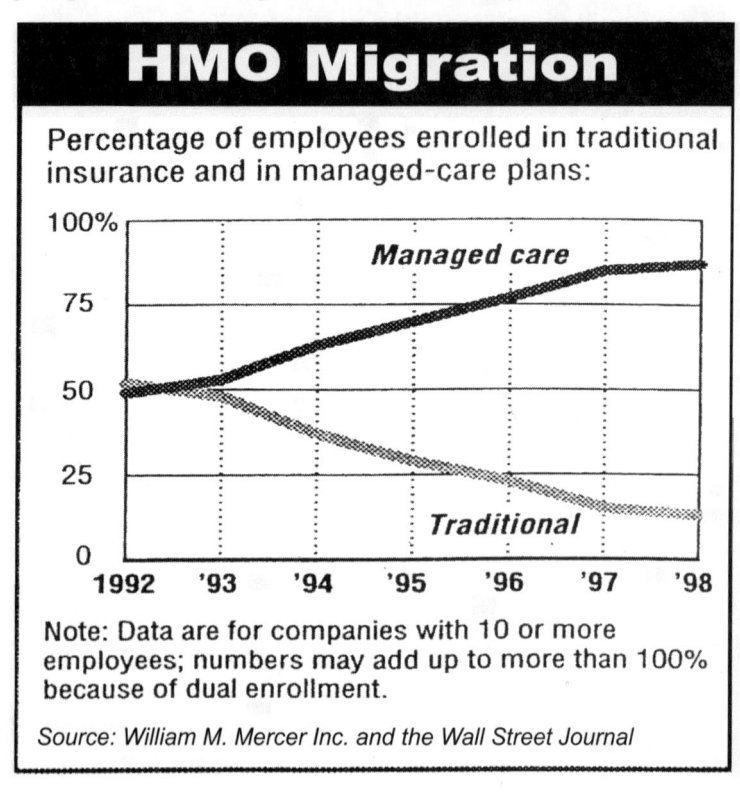

HMO Migration

Percentage of employees enrolled in traditional insurance and in managed-care plans:

Year	Managed care	Traditional
1992	~50%	~50%
'93		
'94		
'95		
'96		
'97		
'98	~85%	~15%

Note: Data are for companies with 10 or more employees; numbers may add up to more than 100% because of dual enrollment.

Source: William M. Mercer Inc. and the Wall Street Journal

There is always going to be a group of people who don't want managed care. The very affluent or people who maybe already have medical conditions that would not be appropriate under managed care. Those folks are probably never going to be in it. So, now it's difficult to grow revenues by adding new members — and that leaves the HMOs with two ways to grow earnings. They can increase the price, or they can cut costs. The pricing strategy has been going well, accounting for about half of revenue growth the past three years — but that doesn't appear sustainable to us over the long term.

Managed Care Increasingly Depends on Pricing

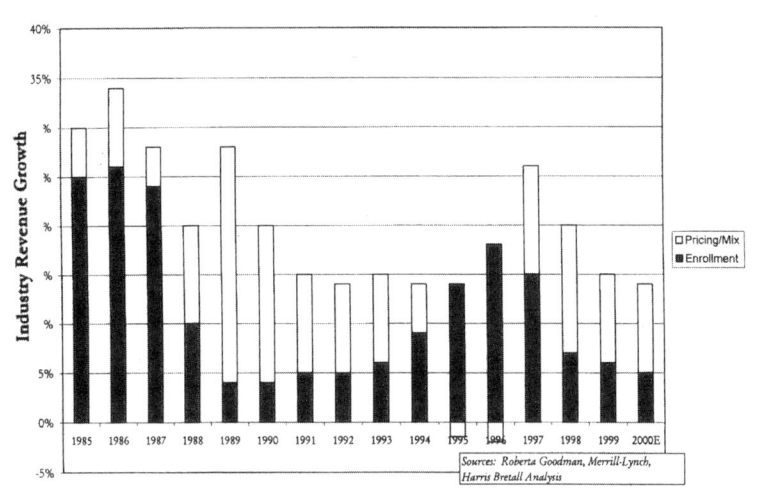

Sources: Roberta Goodman, Merrill-Lynch, Harris Bretall Analysis

Cost-cutting is getting more and more difficult. When an HMO goes to a doctor now and says, "Hey doctor, you're way too expensive. You have to cut your costs for us." The doctor says, "You've been coming to me for 10 years telling me this. I've done your programs and I'm following those practices but I can't cut costs any further without hurting outcomes."

And, at that point the HMOs have a significant problem because it is going to be very difficult to continue to grow earnings. They can't grow membership much, they can't control costs very well, and pricing is not a good long-term strategy. So we are not bullish on this group over the long-term.

There may be some consolidation stories in the group and there might be some trading opportunities there. But, history has shown that mergers are often not positive events. And very few healthcare companies have successfully executed a long-term merger strategy.

150

Knowing what you know about health care, would you encourage your child to be a physician?

I would. I think that the physician's role is changing, and I think that doctors have a unique opportunity to remake their profession, and in a more positive way than many might think.

If a government bureaucrat designs the job of doctor, then it is probably not a job that many talented people will want. But I believe medicine will undergo an incredible transformation over the next 10 to 15 years. Our understanding of human disease — the human genome project, breakthroughs in biotechnology, new treatments for dozens of severe illnesses — will mean there will be a lot of new stuff to learn, and bright and talented people like to learn new things. And physicians will be able to deliver better outcomes in many areas than they have been.

Imagine the opportunities for curing diseases that are currently viewed as hopeless — think about having really effective therapies for Parkinson's or Alzheimer's. Meanwhile, the traditional skills of being an accurate diagnostician and having an intelligent approach to patient therapy are going to be at a real premium. So, it might not be a great time to be a bad doctor but it's a very good time to be an accomplished physician.

151

How is the role of the primary-care physician evolving?

The stereotype used to be that the primary care physician would be a gatekeeper and would ultimately take work away from specialists. I'm sure managed care companies are still telling primary care physicians that you are going to have to learn some orthopedics, optometry or whatever it is going to be. But I doubt if it will work that way in the end. When you think of the volume that is coming down the road with the baby-boom generation, there is going to be a tremendous surge in the number of cases that are going to need to be handled by the system.

There is quite a bit of academic research that shows that once you've identified the health problem, if it's a serious health problem, the best way to handle it is to have someone who is a specialist tackle it. There are plenty of studies that show that high volume providers get better outcomes with things like heart surgeries or hernias – things of that nature. The general practitioner becomes very important as the guy who figures out which center of excellence to send the patient to. And even more important, with patients with diseases like cancer and diabetes, there will probably be a cancer center for excellence and a diabetes center for excellence. Probably, neither of those centers is going to be very good in handling patients who have both diseases, so the GP is going to have to be the one who makes sure the interaction of the two treatment programs doesn't hurt the patient.

152

Which health care companies do you feel have the strongest leadership and best long-term prospects?

We look to invest in companies that innovate, because that's what creates wealth over time. That means we looks for high research and development budgets and strong biotech partnerships. So we like Genentech, Pfizer, and Schering-Plough. Schering-Plough is not the first company people usually think of when we talk about innovation, but we were very impressed with their ability to identify an effective treatment (Rebetron) for Hepatitis C; a major improvement over previous treatments. They accomplished this without spending as much as some of their peers on research and development. But they spent their money very intelligently.

Companies that are able to develop new products in a cost-effective way are going to win. The ones that I think that are most likely to do this are the ones that are already in the process of doing it because it's not an easy skill to learn. Other companies have tried to cut their way to profit and I think that over time those would be disappointing investments.

153

You haven't mentioned Merck.

Merck is a company that we have owned in the past, but we are concerned about their long-term growth prospects.

We don't share the common concern about Merck, which is the patent situation. They will lose patent protection on Vasotec (hypertension), Mevacor (cholesterol), and Prilosec (ulcers), which are all very large drugs. But they are astute managers; and they will have strategies in place to deal with those challenges.

Our concern with Merck is that, as a percentage of pharmaceutical sales, their research and development spending is the lowest of the major players in the U.S. drug industry. We do not think that this is a time where you can get away with shortchanging your research and development efforts, no matter how clever your science people are.

Estimated R&D as a Percentage of 2000E Drug Sales

Major U.S. Pharmaceutical Companies

Pfizer	21.1%
Eli Lilly	20.2%
Pharmacia	17.7%
Johnson & Johnson	15.3%
Schering-Plough	14.3%
Bristol-Myers	13.7%
Glaxo/SmithKline	13.6%
Merck	11.6%

Sources: Company Reports, HBSS Estimates and Analysis

And their pipeline has been disappointing over the last few years. Merck is a great company — they have outstanding people and outstanding researchers, but we are concerned about their ability to deliver new products over time.

154

How are the health care investment prospects outside of the U.S.?

Outside the U.S., the situation becomes more problematic. It is difficult to determine in a general way — you have to think about it on a country-by-country basis. Certainly, the UK drug firms are disappointed with the environment in which they are forced to function. They are looking at merging and even moving operations to the U.S. so they can keep up with their U.S. competitors. There are a number of smaller companies around the world that are developing new compounds. It is in the nature of pharmaceutical research and development that it might come out of a laboratory in Japan or Yugoslavia, but you need to get it to the U.S. market. So what you see are emerging partnerships between U.S. companies and their Japanese companies and European counterparts.

We will see more partnerships, even though some of them have gone sour (I'm thinking of Pfizer and Warner Lambert, which turned into a hostile takeover). The advantages of partnering are too compelling: a small Japanese drug company really is not going to be able to build an effective U.S. sales force. However if they partner with Merck or Pfizer, organizations with good marketing skills, then their product benefits. The marketing organization also benefits by having a broader product portfolio.

155

Do you think that large drug firms, with their big sales forces, are going to change over the next few years by relying more on the Internet and less on an actual sales force calling on physicians?

A lot of people expect that and it could happen, because doctors are people whose time is at such a premium that the Internet is an attractive way to reach them. But the companies that have done the best since the Clinton health care debate are the ones that didn't cut their direct sales forces. Aggressive marketers like Pfizer and Schering-Plough have done relatively well. Companies that de-emphasized marketing have been relative disappointments.

156

What's going to happen to Medicare?

If you look at the polls, people don't feel that the U.S. health care system needs a radical and complete overhaul. But, at the same time, they don't think it needs just a couple of slight changes either. They want to see some substantial changes.

We take it for granted that we will have a Medicare drug benefit. How that benefit will be structured will be very important for the industry. If the prices are set by the government, that could, over the long-term, be a profoundly negative event for the industry, but we think that is very unlikely. I think it's a lot more likely that we'll end up with a Medicare drug benefit that is administered by third-party payers. That may be one opportunity for HMOs to get their enrollment going again. But in any event, we expect to see Medicare drug prices set by the market, not by bureaucrats.

We also expect a move toward more universal coverage. Polls indicate that people view broader coverage as better. They do feel there is something unfair about some Americans having access to good health care and others not having it.

157

Is there anything else that we haven't discussed that we should cover?

You mentioned that a lot of doctors own biotechnology stocks. I think that is a very interesting area — a lot is happening in biotechnology. It has been through such a boom-bust cycle; a real odyssey from a capital markets perspective. There was incredible enthusiasm for biotechnology stocks in the late 1980s and early 1990s. It then faded to complete indifference as it became apparent that a majority of the stocks were not going to be successful and other speculative alternatives appeared, such as the Internet names. There was a multi-year period when there were no major biotech initial public offerings, simply because the capital markets did not want them.

Now we've seen a massive resurgence of interest, which has been fueled by a couple of things. First off from a fundamental standpoint, there used to be two or three profitable biotechnological companies and now there are seven or eight that have crossed over and are now really functional drug companies — like Medimmune or Immunex. They were burning cash a couple years ago and now are generating cash. A company like Genentech, which was not a very exciting stock for a couple of years, has really raised people's eyebrows with the successes that they have had, including the two most successful cancer drug launches in history. Their ability to generate a very large number of promising compounds has surprised everyone to some degree.

I think we will see continued strong interest in biotechnology. But I would caution anyone who wants to get involved in investing in this sector — it is an extremely complex and inefficient market and often biotechnology returns are lottery-like. If you own a hundred companies, ninety of them probably won't work well as investment ideas. But the 10 that do work may work so well that, had you bought all 100 you would still have done better than the market. The PC industry had the same dynamic in the 1980s. There were dozens of PC companies that no one has seen since, but small investments in Microsoft and Intel and maybe Dell or Compaq would have paid for the whole portfolio.

We probably will see that in biotech as we go along. There are many new and interesting therapies that are being developed. But I would warn people not to buy a stock simply because it has a good story. One way that you can verify if a story has validity is if the biotech company has signed up a significant partner. If there is an absence of those partnerships, the investor ought to be careful and ask why.

Another common problem is buying biotech stocks that are running short of cash. Typically, the management of a firm markets the stock more aggressively when they need to raise cash. It's not difficult to go on the Internet and look at how much cash they have and what their short-term investments were in the latest quarter. And look at how quickly they've been burning cash over the years. That's a little bit of due diligence that probably would help most physicians' biotech returns.

158

Do you have any feelings about the movement of doctors to unionize?

I think it is like any other profession. We really don't have lawyer unions, we don't have accountant unions — because it is difficult to take extremely bright, busy people and get them to cooperate on any one matter over a long period of time. The fact is that the doctors' interests diverge from one another among specialties, and even within specialties. So I doubt if much will come of this talk.

Doctors also need to realize how influential they already are. One of the nails in the coffin for managed care was that doctors were angry. When only patients were angry, managed care had a chance. If doctors had said, "hey, there really is something to it — managed care companies are doing a good job managing this" the debate might have tilted in the other direction. But when doctors came out and said these managed health care rules are hurting patient outcomes, that had a big impact.

Doctors should identify situations that are attractive to them as individuals. For some that will mean living in a rural area – if they are willing to sacrifice some of the things that they would get in a larger city, they will probably have more autonomy and get better reimbursement rates relative to the local standard of living than they would get in a larger city.

There are going to be places in this country where it's great to be a doctor and there are going to be places where it's not. Doctors who are in places where it's not should perhaps vote with their feet. We are going to see a situation in this country where medicine will have the potential to be tremendously rewarding. Doctors will be cheating themselves if they don't seek out and track down those favorable situations for themselves.

Interview with Andrew Barrett on Investing in Technology

Andrew Barrett is a frequent guest on national television and radio financial shows where he simplifies and clarifies developments in technology. He informs investors how to invest in this volatile sector. Since 1995, Barrett has been Smith Barney Vice President and Technology Retail Equity Strategist after having worked for several technology companies in Silicon Valley. He earned a joint MBA in Finance and International Business from the Monterey Institute and University of California at Berkeley.

159

What structural economic changes are occurring?

Right now, the economy is going through a major structural upheaval, driven by technology — specifically the Internet. In 1998, our GDP (gross domestic product) growth rate was almost four percent, but if you take out technology's portion, the GDP would have grown a paltry 1.6 percent. Today, technology purchases, as a percentage of non-residential durable equipment spending, is now running about 55 percent. These are basically the products that businesses are buying, and more than half of these purchases are technology.

160

How do you see the Internet affecting our lives and our economy over the next five to 10 years?

In a nutshell, you haven't seen anything yet. The Internet is still in its infancy. The snowball effect is beginning to gain momentum. As devices that can be connected to the Internet become easier to use, and when we are liberated from having to access the Internet via PCs, the changes to our lives and to our society will be even more profound than we have already seen. Non-PC Internet computing devices (cell phones, Palm Pilots, television sets, automobiles or even refrigerators) are now being integrated into the web — and they're going to continue to further break down barriers to entry. This will proliferate the spread and flow of information, increase the availability of choices and options, and speed the time and efficiency of markets and things in our daily lives. It's going to be pretty amazing.

161

The price/earnings ratios (P/E ratios) of information technology stocks are many times those of the S&P 500. Do you believe this difference is justified?

P/E ratios are not an effective way to measure Internet stocks. Most information technology is now considered intellectual capital, and P/Es are not a good reflection of intellectual capital. When we talk about things like automobiles or toasters, which are actual, physical products, then we use a P/E ratio. If we talk about intellectual goods or things that are intangible, then we look at price to growth rates or price to sales. So, P/Es are not really effective tools, and the current high P/E is probably justified.

162

Many states and municipalities are losing significant tax revenues on sales made on the Internet. A consumer who buys a book at a local bookstore must pay local sales tax. If this consumer buys the same book from amazon.com. or barnesandnoble.com., no sales tax is charged. How long will this sales tax disparity be permitted?

I think the federal government is going to keep out of the Internet taxation question and leave it to individual states to decide. Many states have experienced a loss of revenue due to the disparity and would like to do something about it; however, no state wants to be the first to levy an Internet tax. So, it's a question of when each state can gain enough members or enough of a consensus to implement an Internet sales tax. My guess is that we will not see this legislation passed for several years. When it is, I think it will have only a minor impact on consumer Internet spending. The studies that we've seen estimate that it would shave 15 percent of business-to-consumer e-commerce revenues. We think that's a negligible amount considering the growth in the industry.

163

What is the next wave of technology from which investors can expect to profit?

The next wave that technology investors are going to profit from is simply a refocusing away from the Y2K remediation efforts that we saw between 1995 to1999, and toward web strategies, e-business strategies and a general upgrade of software systems. For the next two or three years, we're going to see a tremendous amount of pent-up demand by U.S. corporations to implement new technologies that are now liberated from Y2K efforts.

164

You have frequently mentioned the seasonal nature of technology stocks. How can investors benefit from this knowledge in constructing their portfolios?

Investors need to recognize that technology stocks are inherently seasonal and go through some observed swings throughout the year. Once investors understand this, then they can better identify the best times to add to portfolios and lighten portfolios. It also helps to understand when the markets are moving, because the media consistently misinterprets these seasonal cycles as fundamental concerns. Two major seasonal factors affect technology. The first is a summertime slowdown, which has been dubbed the "ice-cream effect." It causes technology to under perform around May, and generally from August through September. Then, in October, we see a seasonal upswing that we call the "Santa-Claus effect" or the "holiday effect," when sales are very strong, and technology does very well. So, investors can play around with these two seasonal moves, adding to positions around September and October and taking some profits in the peaks around January.

165

What are the fundamental drivers of technology?

There are several major drivers for technology. The first is the earnings growth rate. Right now, on a worldwide basis, the technology sector is expected to grow by nine percent annually for the next few years. Certain areas within technology, namely software and datacom equipment, are going to grow more. The projected annual growth rate for software is 14 percent and for datacom is 11.4 percent. The second major driver is the evolution of the economy into the technology or digital age. More and more of our economy is now being represented by technology. We think that is going to continue as we move forward. Right now, technology roughly represents 12 percent of our economy and we expect that to grow to 20 to 25 percent by 2005. The third major driver is productivity enhancement. In late 1992, we crossed the line when manufacturing compensation per hour exceeded unit labor costs. Since then, productivity gains per hour have been dwarfing unit labor costs, and that is going to continue to drive new deployment.

I think the last area is the product cycle. The product cycle for technology, in our eyes, is one of the best ways to gauge the future and identify the major drivers. For the next two years, we see the product cycles at probably the most robust we have seen them in their known existence.

166

What happened to the classic economic theory — you can't have four percent GDP growth with less than five percent unemployment without creating wage-price pressures and inflation?

Federal Reserve governor Allan Greenspan threw that out the window in 1999 when he said that he is comfortable with four percent GDP growth going back to the issue of productivity. The classic example, as you correctly point out, is that you would instantly hit inflation with four percent GDP growth. But now that your labor costs have come down so dramatically and your productivity enhancements have allowed this, you can grow much faster without the risk of wage-inflation, which typically precludes general inflation.

167

Who will be the survivors of the Internet IPOs?

The attributes of a winning Internet company are clear vision, terrific management, a defined brand, an early time to market and a bulletproof execution strategy. Companies that display these attributes will ultimately be the winners. There are a lot of companies out there with very exciting business plans but absolutely no way of executing them, and they are the ones I don't think will do well. So, when you look at an Internet IPO, typically in this market, the stock will go up on its first day, because of the sizzle surrounding it. But, you have to cut through all of the fanfare and press releases, and look at where the company is and at its competitive landscape. If it has a dominant market share, this is a positive sign. We look to see if it sticks to its core competencies and concentrates on those areas it does best. If it has a vertical structure instead of a horizontal structure, meaning that it offers many different services within that core competency, and doesn't branch out to many different areas. And we look at management, because management is probably the ultimate determining factor of which Internet companies will survive.

168

What changes will occur in cellular service over the next five to 10 years?

What we have seen in cellular services over the past five years has been a migration from analog to digital technology. It has been a pretty powerful trend for a lot of companies. The next big wave is the migration from digital to voice to data. We have several different technologies, wireless application protocol being one of them, moving on into the next generation or the third generation of wireless, called 3G. 3G is going to have powerful data transfer capabilities and will allow many different devices to surf the web, send emails and the like. So, the build-up is going to continue, and voice technology is going to be dwarfed by the proliferation of data technology.

169

Any comments on day trading? Online trading?

Most of the day traders have formed a little niche in their markets. And I think day trading is going to continue to be around, although not in as glamorous a light as the media has portrayed it. On line trading continues to proliferate because it is an effective medium and the markets are becoming inherently efficient. One thing that we found in the surveys that we have done is that while consumers are continuing to find the best value, they will continue to pay money for intelligence. I think you will find, in the financial services, that intelligence will be stressed over execution. Anybody can trade stocks. I think what you will find more, in terms of retail ownership and participation in the market, will be under a money-management type of environment, not in an individual transactional environment.

170

Why are most Internet companies unprofitable? Will online media advertising expenditures transform many of the unprofitable Internet companies?

Most Internet companies don't make a profit simply because every single dime that they make has got to be plowed back into the business in an effort to gain market share. As we said earlier, branding and market share are essential. Online media advertising expenditures are actually going to increase to levels that many people don't expect. Why? In an effort to gain market share and brand awareness, companies need to discount their products or advertise their products. Both of these strategies are going to continue. So, traditional advertising media like TV, radio, and billboards are going to benefit, as will online advertising, which is going to eat up more and more market share of overall advertising budgets.

171

We've discussed the effect of technology on the U.S. economy. What effect will it have on the global economy? And what effect will it have on third world nations with commodity-based economies?

Technology implementation in the U.S. has lead to our productivity, our low inflation, and our extremely powerful GDP growth. We are now seeing a worldwide recovery that's leading to the deployment of technology. Right now, Europe is about two years behind the U.S. in certain areas in terms of technology deployment and in business technology. In terms of telecommunications, they could be as much as three to four years behind us. So, there's a lot of catch-up work that needs to be done. Asia is in a similar boat. They are coming out of a pretty strong downturn in their economy. They're behind in their infrastructure deployment, so as the rest of the world begins to ramp up I think growth in Asia will surpass our domestic growth. As a result, many companies will find that their most profitable growth opportunities will be outside the United States. I think that bodes extremely well in terms of low worldwide inflation and increased productivity. It also bodes well for technology stocks and services. As for third world nations with commodity-based economies, technology improves order, transfer flow, and the ability to automate processes — especially in manufacturing quality control. This just basically lowers a company's cost to produce and increases its competitiveness.

172

You have written, "Over the last five years, the tech sector has lead the market in average, year-over-year quarterly growth," How long do you feel this trend will continue?

I think if we look at year-over-year growth, at some point you are going to have to see some degree of slow-down. That's simply a function of the law of big numbers. If we look at where technology is positioned in relation to the rest of the economy, it looks like both technology and telecommunications companies, for the next 12 months, are positioned to continue to outpace the rest of the market. Therefore, they will probably lead the market in terms of share price and performance. Looking out even further, I think we'll still see continued growth because of continued worldwide expansion. But that growth will probably be slower than previous levels.

173

What is broadband? What benefits will it bring? What changes will it create?

Broadband is simply the widening of the pipes into the home. Right now the vast majority of American homes, even European homes, are wired for 56 kilobit, meaning standard analog modems which are transported over voice lines. Broadband expands this and allows megabits per second worth of high-speed data to come into home and allow the individual very high speed, very interactive, Internet experiences. Broadband technology can be used in several different ways, one of which is the cable modem.

Another way is via a Digital Subscriber Line (DSL), which is an amplified, augmented phone line. The third is via a wireless or a satellite link. Broadband is going to bring enormous amounts of web experiences to consumers, thereby, increasing the use of the web. Thereby, necessitating the need for more web infrastructure. I think that it is going to change the way investors and consumers treat the web. Instead of a novelty that has access by a PC, the web will be a true working medium, which allows all of the things in the home to connect themselves online and everything to be interconnected via wireless or cable systems.

174

How can investors profit from broadband?

The best way to profit from broadband is via a basket of names, because there are several technologies being deployed. I think investors should look at buying some of the backbone companies that are providing the raw data. I also think that you should also look at some of the equipment manufacturers on the backbone. You can look at some of the deliverers on the content side. The cable companies are a very good way to play this. You want to look at some of the "in the home" areas. The phone companies are very well positioned. You also want to consider some cable/modem provider services. And finally, you want to look at some of the semi-conductor names that are used to power all of these things.

175

What percentage of a 40-year-old physician's investment and retirement portfolio should consist of tech stocks?

Currently I recommend an overweight position within the technology, and that would roughly represent about 22 or 23 percent of a portfolio in techs and about 20 percent in telecommunications.

176

A 65-year-old physician is getting ready to retire. What percentage of his/her portfolio should consist of tech stocks?

I think we would do two things. I think we would scale that down to maybe a total of 10 percent to15 percent in technology and 15 percent in telecommunications. We would also upgrade the names in the portfolio to make sure that they owned the core-tech and telecom names.

177

What about computer manufacturers?

I don't think that those are cores. They are just too cyclical.

178

What will replace the Internet?

I don't think anything replaces the Internet. It just gets changed into something that is more user-friendly and ubiquitous. The Internet simply becomes an open highway, where any sort of data, voice or video, anything can move anywhere onto any device seamlessly and effortlessly — with almost zero cost and zero barriers.

179

Is there anything you wish to add?

I think that the proliferation of Internet is going to necessitate the need for several sectors. Investors should understand that while technology has a very strong upward growth trend, not all tech stocks are going to go up. Investors must remain focused on certain areas. The focus areas that we like as we move into the new millennium include of course Internet infrastructure, Internet service companies, wireless companies, semiconductors and software. We think that if investors focus their efforts in those areas, they will be highly rewarded.

Chapter 4
Planning for Retirement

Isn't it strange how time moves faster when we are in our forties than when we are in our twenties or thirties? It's even stranger how much faster time seems to fly when we are in our fifties or sixties than when we were in our forties. We can no longer depend upon our employers to provide for comfortable retirements.

Fewer employers are providing defined benefit plans or pensions to their employees. Instead, defined contribution plans such as 401(k) and 403(b) plans are offered, where the employee and not the employer is responsible for ensuring his/her funding for retirement. Under these plans, you — not your employer — are solely responsible for selecting the right investments to adequately fund your retirement.

With increased longevity, the greatest financial concern facing most retirees is outliving your money because of inflation. I also write a personal finance column for law enforcement organizations in Florida. Many law enforcement and military personnel retire in their forties and early fifties. When I tell them in seminars or individual meetings that they may possibly spend more time retired than they spend working, I get puzzled looks. Since these very early retirees may be spending 40 years being retired, they need to increase their nest eggs during retirement fourfold just to maintain purchasing power. Those retiring in their sixties need to triple their nest eggs to stay ahead of inflation during retirement.

The key to staying ahead of inflation is to have your assets grow faster than the inflation rate. Playing it too safe by investing retirement money in CDs, bonds, bond funds and money market funds will offer no guarantee against loss of purchasing power.

Physicians, like everybody else, are concerned about making a smooth transition when they retire. Many consult with Dr.Gigi Hirsch, M.D., a psychiatrist and former Harvard Medical School instructor. Following this chapter is an interview with Dr. Hirsch. She discusses how she advises physicians on personal career issues such as preparing for retirement, avoiding malpractice suits from patients, and reenergizing their careers.

180

Should I be investing for income when I retire next year at age 62?

No! If you're like the average American, you could be spending 20-30 years retired — and that means you will need to at least triple your income during retirement just to stay ahead of increased costs. The key to never outliving your money is to invest primarily for growth, and to make systematic withdrawals at a rate less than the growth rate of your portfolio. If you invest primarily for income, you paint yourself into a corner. Your nest egg will not be growing; inflation is reducing its purchasing power. Time works against you.

181

What kind of retirement planning is most popular with Americans?

When I first heard Jonathan Pond (noted author of more than 11 books on personal financial planning) ask this question on public television, I was sure the answer would be Individual Retirement Accounts (IRAs) or 401(k) plans. And I was wrong on both counts! Would you believe that more Americans buy lottery tickets than invest in retirement plans? And when these lottery ticket hopefuls were asked what they would do IF (not when) they win, most said that they would stop working and retire!

182

I am 67 years old. Will my Social Security benefits be reduced if I take a part-time job?

No, after your 65th birthday you are entitled to full Social Security benefits, no matter how much income you earn. The earnings test was repealed in 2000 for Social Security recipients age 65-70 regardless of the amount of their earned income.

183

Is borrowing from a 401(k) retirement plan advisable?

No. Did you know that if you have to leave your company because you retired, were laid off, or were fired, you would be required to pay any outstanding loan balances immediately? And if you can't, you'll have to pay ordinary income taxes on the amount you owe plus a 10 percent penalty for premature withdrawal (if you are not over 55 when you leave your job). Borrowing from your 401(k) plan is like mortgaging your retirement plan. I recommend that you avoid doing it.

184

When I retire in two years at the age of 64, should I be supporting myself from mutual funds in my retirement account or my taxable account?

Normally, if you are in the 28 percent tax bracket or above, it is advisable to withdraw from your taxable account first. This lets your retirement account continue to grow tax deferred until you have to begin taking mandatory distributions at age 70-1/2.

185

I am 71 years old and still working full-time and taking mandatory withdrawals from my Keogh. Am I still permitted to contribute to my Keogh?

Yes, as long as you have self-employment income. Individuals aged 70 and over, with annual income may contribute to retirement plans — Keoghs, SEP's, 401(k), 403(b), and profit sharing. Exception: You are not allowed to contribute to a traditional IRA once you reach 70 — but a Roth IRA is okay if your adjusted gross income is within income limitations.

186

I am 59, in private practice and hope to continue working for five to 10 more years. I have half of my retirement funds in money market. Is this a wise decision?

No, not in my opinion. According to Ibbotson Associates of Chicago, annual returns from large company stocks averaged 11.3 percent and small company stocks averaged 12.6 percent over the past 74 years. If you wish to average a 10 percent annual return in your existing portfolio and one half is earning less than five percent, the other half needs to earn in excess of 15 percent which is not realistic. With a five to 10 year investment time horizon, I recommend not leaving half of your portfolio in money market. If you are not comfortable investing mostly in growth, consider a balanced portfolio consisting of equities and fixed income.

187

a. Being a self-employed physician, is there a maximum limit that I am allowed to contribute to a Keogh retirement plan?

The lesser of $ 30,000 or 25 percent of earned income is the maximum contribution limit for a Keogh.

b. I have seen tables where Keogh accounts can grow to $32 million in 40 years. What is the catch?

The catch is the wonder of compounding. If you invest $30,000 in your Keogh at the start of each year and continue for 40 years achieving an annual 12.75 percent rate of return, the market value of this account will be $32 million before taxes and inflation.

188

My financial consultant told me that I should be concerned about my cash flow, and not my income, during my retirement (which starts next year). What does she mean?

She may be trying to tell you that the amount of money you actually receive each month from your overall investments (your cash-flow) is what supports you. For example, if your investments are growing 10 percent annually (through appreciation, dividends and interest) and you are systematically withdrawing six to seven percent annually, you have a positive cash flow. Your financial consultant is wisely trying to ensure that you do not outlive your money.

Let's assume your portfolio's average annual growth of 10 percent is made up of three percent in dividends/interest and seven percent price appreciation. Then, the income from your investments would only be three percent. Many retirees make the mistake of becoming preoccupied with the income component of their portfolio and ignore the growth component. Income investments offer no protection against inflation, which may be one of the greatest threat to the financial well-being of retirees.

189

Can creditors seize my Keogh plans?

No, there is an ERISA prohibition against "assignment or alienation of benefits." IRAs do not have this protection. In some states, IRAs may be protected from creditors. Before rolling assets from a Keogh plan to an IRA, you may wish to consult a local attorney.

190

My wife and I are each 66 years old. We have $3,000,000 in a tax-free bond fund and live in a mortgage-free home valued at $600,000. I plan to retire this year. We don't wish to leave an estate; rather, we want to maximize our stream of income while we're alive. I'm assuming that we each have a life expectancy of 18 years, that the annual inflation rate will be 3.5 percent, and that our tax-free yield will be 5.5 percent. How much money can we take out of our bond fund each year?

If we make these assumptions, you'll have an annual income (adjusted for a 3.5 percent inflation rate) of $198,918 for 18 years. This strategy is designed to deplete your nest egg so that the day the second of you die exactly at age 84, you're completely broke. But what happens if you and/or your wife live to be 95? Sound far-fetched? It's not. According to demographic studies, one out of five people lives to be 95 these days. A better choice may be to buy a single premium immediate annuity with the $3,000,000 that provides you with an annual income of approximately $230,000 for as long as you or your wife lives. After the second of the two of you dies, the annuity stops paying and is terminated. This way, you and your wife will never outlive your money.

191

My medical group is taking part in a Supplemental Executive Retirement Plan (SERP). My knowledge of this plan is quite limited and even my accountant had to do some research to see what these plans were all about. Can you tell me something about the pros and cons?

A SERP is a type of deferred compensation plan that is unfunded but set up only for specially selected employees. This plan is generally exempt from ERISA (Employee Retirement Income Security Act of 1974) regulations. ERISA comprises the massive and complicated federal laws covering retirement and pension laws. If you leave this group for whatever reason, your SERP benefits are not portable and must be paid out to you. This will create immediate income subject to ordinary income taxes and may push you to a higher tax bracket. Since A SERP is exempt from ERISA and does not have its protections, it may be subject to creditor claims.

192

I'm a family physician (age 52) and plan to retire at 65. I have a six percent fixed annuity that has grown to $320,000. I've rolled it over in the past 15 years three times after the penalty expiration. Do you think this is a good investment to fund my retirement?

No, I think you need to get a much better annual return than 6 percent on your retirement nest egg. I recommend you convert your fixed annuity into a variable annuity. It's a tax-free exchange under Internal Revenue Code (IRC) 1035 (also called a 1035 Exchange). Use a top-quality insurance company and invest in a conservatively balanced fund of equities and bonds within the variable annuity. With most variable annuities, the $320,000 principal will be guaranteed to your heirs. If you don't wish to invest the entire amount in the equity market all at once, you may dollar cost average or invest 1/6 or 1/12 in growth monthly. If the markets drop while you are dollar cost averaging, the share price is less and you are rewarded with more shares. Let's compare the results at your 65th birthday using both types of annuities. Over the next 13 years, the $320,000 fixed annuity (averaging six percent annually) would grow to $682,537 while the variable annuity (averaging 10 percent annually) would grow to $1,104,726.

193

I have been out of residency and in private practice for almost one year. I've paid off my credit cards and my debt now consists of one car loan, the mortgage on my house and school loans. At the end of each month, there is a small amount left after paying all the bills and I want to invest it for my future. There are so many possibilities that I don't know where to begin. Should I contribute more to my 401(k); invest in mutual funds, T-bills, or the stock market; or pay off my school loans more quickly?

Pay yourself first by contributing to your 401(k) plan. This money will be automatically deducted from your pay and will reduce your taxable income. Make sure you invest only in growth investments; domestic (75 percent) and international (25 percent) and not in money market or bonds. I would also shop for a qualified financial advisor so that you can concentrate on building a successful medical practice. Do what you do best and hire out the rest!

194

When my ex-wife died, the value of our children's custodial accounts was included in her estate and subject to estate taxes. Why were they included in her estate when they were Uniform Gifts To Minors Act accounts and were in the children's social security numbers?

Because your wife was the custodian for these accounts and controlled them, the value of these accounts was treated as if it were in her estate.

195

Where did the number 401(k) for my retirement plan come from?

From the Internal Revenue Code (IRC) detailing a section of a retirement plan. For example IRC, Section 401 (k) deals with salary reduction defined contribution plans, Section 403 (b) is for non-profit organizations and Section 457 is for governmental employees.

196

I am trying to find a good software program for calculations for retirement possibilities. I am 48, married and have $1.5 million in personal savings and $1.5 million in retirement accounts. How soon can I retire assuming that I need $120,000 annual income after taxes and eight percent annual return with three percent annual inflation rate?

Instead of a software program; I use a financial calculator (HP 12C). For calculation purposes, I would disregard Social Security potential income and assume 28 percent tax bracket with 1/2 income derived from retirement (ERISA) accounts under substantial and equal payments. This permits you to access these accounts and start taking distributions before age 59-1/2 without being subjected to a 10 percent premature distribution penalty.

You can actually start retiring now and based upon your assumptions, take $160,856 gross annual distributions and not run out of money until your 100th birthday. What's the problem? You need to build in an inflation protector and portfolio protector by having long term care insurance for you and your wife with a compound inflation rider. You'll also need a good health insurance policy until Medicare kicks in.

197

How did you arrive at this figure?

Using a HP 12C financial calculator, first calculate your minimum required annual income. From retirement account $60,000 divided by .72 (ERISA after tax payment) + personal savings account $60,000 = $143,833 minimum required annual income. Now we input the following data on the financial calculator:

Press Begin payments

Interest (I) = 1.08 divided by 1.03-1 times 100 = 4.8543 percent; this is your eight percent return adjusted for three percent inflation.

Number of years (n) = 42 (100 - current age 48)

Present Value (PV) = 3,000,000 (change sign)

Future Value (FV) = 0 (at age 10)

Find payment (pmt) = $160,856; since this amount is greater than $143,833 (minimum required annual income), you are able to begin retirement today!

198

What do you think of the rule of thumb of subtracting your age from 100, and keeping that percentage of your portfolio in stocks and the remainder in bonds?

I don't agree with a one size fits all investment strategy since individuals have different financial, personal, health and family issues. Using this rule of thumb, a 40-year-old should have 60 percent of his/her portfolio in equities and 40 percent in bonds even though he/she may be 25 years away from retirement, have a moderate-to-high risk tolerance and live for 40-50 more years.

Interview with Dr. Gigi Hirsch on the Changing Healthcare Industry

Dr. Gigi Hirsch, M.D. completed her residency training in internal medicine and psychiatry and was an Instructor in Psychiatry at Harvard Medical School from 1992-1997. She helps physicians strategically manage their careers in the rapidly changing healthcare industry. She also helps physician employers and those manufacturing products for use by physicians to better understand what tools and supports that physicians need in their practices and their careers. Dr. Hirsch's work has been featured in the *Wall Street Journal, National Public Radio's All Things Considered* and *Marketplace.* I learned about her while driving home from work and hearing her being interviewed on *Marketplace.* Hirsch's book, *Strategic Career Management for the 21st Century Physician,* published by the American Medical Association, was sold out from pre-sales before its release in January 2000.

199

What do you do?

I am the founder and CEO of a consulting and research firm based in Boston called MDIntellinet. The focus of our work at MDIntellinet is the management of physician human capital — how to develop it, manage it, and leverage it to its full potential. We believe that physicians represent a pool of very valuable knowledge workers within the healthcare industry ... an industry that must become much more adept at managing resources. Physicians are an asset pool that is not currently being optimally leveraged in the industry. MDIntelliNet studies that factors that contribute to and result from this, and addresses them through a range of consulting and web-based services.

200

How long have you been doing this?

I have been doing this since 1992. At that time on was on the faculty of Harvard Medical School and I received a grant from Beth Israel Hospital to launch and run a new national nonprofit research and consulting organization called The Center for Physician Development, which was the predecessor of MD Intellinet.

201

Before starting your own company, you worked as an emergency room physician in Boston. How did you like being an emergency room physician?

Initially I enjoyed the variety and pace of the work. I also found it interesting and challenging. After about five years of working in emergency medicine, my interests began to shift and focus on systems issues that relate to how physicians are trained and supported in their work, and how these factors impact patient care. I decided that I wanted to broaden my sphere of influence beyond working one-on-one with patients so that I could help to shape these systems.

202

How many physician clients do you have?

I have provided individual career consultations to more than 1,500 physicians. Through speaking engagements and consultations to provider organizations, I have had contact with many more physicians. We probably have a total of 6,000 physicians in our database who have taken the initiative to contact us either by phone or through our website over the years for information and services.

203

Do you communicate with all of these physicians face-to-face or electronically?

It's a combination of face-to-face, electronic and telephone contact. Approximately 90 percent of the consultations with physicians that I do are by telephone.

204

What motivates physicians to contact you?

They are motivated to contact MDIntelliNet by range of types of career issues. They may call us when:
- They are planning their retirement.
- They are looking for a new job either within patient care or perhaps a more nontraditional area of the market — for example in pharmaceuticals or e-health.
- They are looking for part-time career opportunities to increase the variety in their clinical work, or to bring in additional revenues alongside of their active practice.
- They are considering pursuing an additional graduate degree like a MPH or an MBA.

Some of them call us because their malpractice or disability insurance companies have referred them to us. Doctors who are in the midst of a malpractice suit or who are on disability often either want to, or need to, consider a career transition.

205

What do these clients hope that you can accomplish for them?

Our physician clients often call us because they are seeking general information about career trends in the industry that might be relevant to their personal situation. Most physicians feel as though they live and work in a bit of a vacuum. They are so busy and insulated in their daily lives that they are unable to see broader career perspectives in the profession. Also, within the medical culture, most physicians do not openly discuss personal career issues . . . physicians are very private.

Clients also come to us for expert guidance on their career planning, as well as defining their networking and marketing strategies. They may be medical students trying to decide which specialty to pursue; or they may be in clinical practice and interested in more aggressively marketing their expert witness services to law firms; or they may have a new business idea and hoping that we can link them with appropriate business development resources.

Sometimes they come to us hoping that we can link them with specific job opportunities, and sometimes they are looking more for a mentor or coach to be available over time to them.

206

You also consult for companies in technology, healthcare and insurance sectors. How do you help these companies?

Our work with companies outside of the clinical services sector focuses in better leveraging of physician intellectual capital. We help these companies get quick, targeted access to physicians for market research, or for alpha (early stage of product development) or beta (later development) testing of new technology products. We sometimes put together a specialty group of physicians to serve as an advisory panel to a company for a particular issue or product. Whenever possible we also try to create new part-time opportunities and project-based work for physicians in industry. These types of arrangements are a valuable way for industry to leverage physician expertise and contacts without taking on the cost and challenges associated with hiring physicians on a full-time basis.

207

What is the most gratifying aspect of what you do?

I guess there are two things that I find gratifying. One, when I am able to help physicians connect or reconnect with their passions as they relate to their careers, especially after they have reached a point in their career where they felt they were stagnating or under stimulated. It's very exciting to watch them blossom.

On the other side of the fence in the industry, it's very exciting for me to have the ear of high-level industry executives and be able to effectively educate them about a broader range of ways that they might be working with physicians in order to develop and sell more successful products.

208

Any suggestions for physicians to avoid malpractice suits from patients?

A lot of malpractice suits do not really result from bad or negligent care. Many of the suits actually are rooted in communication problems that exist between the physician and patient and possibly the patient's family. As stress and burnout symptoms mount for physicians, it makes them more vulnerable to the kinds of communication problems that relate to irritability and frustration. It reduces their ability to be patient and empathic with a person, which is sometimes called compassion fatigue. I think that if physicians notice these symptoms creeping into their daily work, they need to find a way of stepping back, reflecting and contemplating changes in their careers so that they can relieve these symptoms. If they don't, they are at increased risk of malpractice suits.

Our research at MDIntelliNet suggests that physicians suffering from prolonged stress and burnout are at higher risk for a number of morbid outcomes — not just malpractice suits, but also disability claims, medical errors, and turnover of staff and patients, among others.

209

Are physicians retiring earlier?

Yes, many of the physicians are retiring earlier than they ever expected they would. Although many of them don't want to become totally inactive professionally, they just want to leave the daily grind of direct patient care as it is being practiced today. I haven't seen a whole lot of data on this but I do know that the recruiting firm of Merritt, Hawkins & Assoc. did a survey of physicians that were at least 50 years old. The results of this survey showed that 38 percent planned to retire in the next three years while an additional 10 percent were planning to change to a new career in the very near future. Also the American College of Radiology reported that retirement has doubled between the years of 1995 and 1998.

210

From your consulting observations, what are the challenges facing physicians who have been in practice five to 10 years?

One of the patterns I notice is about that time frame that physicians tend to reach a certain level of technical mastery. Up until that time, their energy is focused on making sure that they know how to practice their technical specialty adequately and a lot of their anxiety relates to making a technical mistake.

Between five to 10 years of practicing medicine, physicians achieve a certain level of mastery so that simply practicing their technical specialty doesn't require as much active mental energy. For many physicians that is the first time in their career that they have really stopped to reflect on their future and where their career may be heading. Many will begin to think about some sort of additional career diversification activity — such as pursuing a part-time graduate degree in public health, or getting involved in a clinical research project. Others may decide that they are feeling restless and even bored in their work, and they want to make some type of a major transition, for example, into a full-time job in the pharmaceutical industry. At that point in the career counseling that I do, I will often encourage them to develop a niche or area of expertise in which to begin marketing themselves as experts.

211

What about the challenges facing physicians with 20 to 30-plus years experience who may be getting ready for retirement?

For them, it's often a question of what is the exit mode is going to be — are they going to cut back to part time or completely exit their career in medicine.

Many recognize their sense of isolation and how one-dimensional their life has become in medicine. The fact that they don't really have any hobbies and there is nothing that they really know how to do or have wanted to do besides taking care of patients. This is such a fundamental part of their identity, their medical practice is the psychological glue that holds them together. The thought of retirement can be very frightening to them. As per your last question, if after their first five to 10 years in practice they had successfully established a non-clinical niche area of expertise, and had marketed themselves well in this niche, they would likely have some post-retirement career opportunities related to this.

212

You work with physicians who are referred to you as troublemakers. Please explain.

There are a number of provider organizations that send physicians to me when they are causing trouble of some sort. Often, the problems related to temper outbursts or other types of "acting out" behavior by the physician. Often I find through meeting with this individuals that the underlying problem relates to a "bad fit" between the physician and the organizational work environment that they are in. A bad fit can result from a general incompatibility of the values and work style of the individual and the organization. For example, an individual who is very independent and control-oriented is not likely to be happy practicing in an organization which micromanages its physicians.

As physicians, we are not taught about organizational behavior and culture, or how to evaluate an organization as a potential work setting for our practice. It often takes very little contemplation to see that a particular individual and a particular organization are not likely to mesh well . . . it's just that there in many cases there is little systematic attention from either party to these kinds of issues at the time the hiring takes place.

213

Would you explain how isolation is preventing many physicians from being more effective?

There is a lot less time these days for curbside consults between physicians in practice. If one physician has a challenging case that he/she wants to run by another physician, there is rarely an opportunity to do that anymore. These used to be commonplace, and added to the quality of care, as well as the intellectual stimulation and satisfaction of practice.

214

Many physicians are financially squeezed or trapped because of sizable student loans and significant financial obligations incurred prior to major pay cuts. Any comments?

Yes, this is a frequent occurrence. I think that financial pressures often influence people to select a particular specialty that appears to pay well. In addition, some individual recognize at a certain point in their career that they made the wrong specialty choice, or even the wrong profession. However, outstanding debts from training can lead them to feel that they cannot afford to make a transition that might be more suitable.

215

Nurses can be cross-trained on the job. What about physicians?

Nurses have a broader range of lateral career mobility and options than physicians. In order for physicians to make a lateral career change, it usually requires complete retraining which is at least a two to three year process.

216

Let's assume you have been invited to give a commencement address to a medical school graduating class. What advice would you give these brand new doctors?

I would orient my advice around the concept of the physician's "Career Ecosystem" — a concept that has evolved through my consultations with physicians over the years. The Career Ecosystem consists of three primary sphere of their work life that all require care and attention: the Personal, the Professional, and the Organizational spheres.

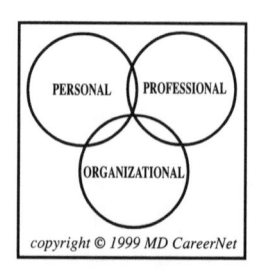

[Venn diagram showing three overlapping circles labeled PERSONAL, PROFESSIONAL, and ORGANIZATIONAL. copyright © 1999 MD CareerNet]

A major shift in any one of these spheres tends to cause direct or indirect shifts in the others. Thus, they truly operate as an "ecosystem," meaning that they exist in synergistic and interdynamic ways.

Maintaining equilibrium in the ecosystem requires care and attention throughout one's career lifecycle. For this occasion, I would want to make one suggestion that relates to each of these spheres.

In the Professional sphere I would recommend that everyone pursue one non-clinical skill set alongside his/her clinical skill set. Now that may take the form of being involved with clinical research or getting involved in software development in medicine. It's very important to have this tandem skill set that does not involve patient care. This helps prevent physician burnout and ensures employability in the unfortunate event that the individual becomes sick or disabled and can no longer practice direct patient care.

In the Organizational sphere, I would stress the importance of the fit between the organization and the individual. Many physicians don't recognize the importance of the work environment — how it shapes the daily conditions of their work and influences their daily work satisfaction. I would encourage them not to take the first job they are offered but to talk with people who work within a range of types of organizational settings to try gain insight into what type of organization might provide the best "fit" for them.

In the Personal sphere, I would communicate the reality that during your training as a physician, it's crucial that you live with a certain denial of your needs. It gets down to basic survival in your training. You don't notice hunger, exhaustion (the need to get sleep) — these things are essential for your survival in training but you need to undo this training as soon as you graduate. It is crucial that you regain the ability to be in touch with yourself and know how to recognize your needs in the long haul. This is fundamental to protecting your ability to take good care of your patients and to preventing your own burnout.

217

Do you see any positive changes coming from this era of managed care?

I think that when I first began doing this work about a decade ago, the term career management didn't really exist. We talked about professional development but not career management. I think managed care has created enough exquisite pain across the industry that physicians are now more openly discussing career issues. It has brought many career management issues out of the closet-these issues are much more openly discussed now than they have ever been discussed in the past. A lot of the issues that are being discussed have to do with managed care but a lot transcend the era of managed care. This gives us the opportunity to look at issues that are timeless in career management of physicians.

In addition, there are a number of physicians who are interested in becoming managers and administrators in medicine and more of those opportunities have opened up with the restructuring of managed care. Also managed care has required that we practice medicine in fundamentally different ways, for better or for worse. That has created the need for new kinds of products in the industry, and — along with these — a broader range of roles that physicians can play in industry if they are interested.

218

How can medical schools prepare physicians for careers?

Although it is hard to believe, medical students and residents still do not get good, practical career guidance during their training. Despite the major financial and life investment that students make in their professional training, they are still not provided with the guidance they need to help them make well-informed career decisions. As a result, many misguided decisions are made that have painful and long-lasting consequences. Unfortunately, with all of the pressures on medical schools these days, I don't expect that good career counseling is something that we are likely to see provided anytime soon, especially because the schools are not in any way held accountable for outcomes in this arena as in other areas.

Chapter 5
All About IRAs

During the past 10 years, there has been a major shift, not only in wealth, but also in wealth composition. The largest single asset most physicians owned used to be their personal residences. With the bull market of the past decade, the value of many physicians' retirement accounts has exceeded the value of their homes. Frequently these retirement accounts have been rolled over into individual retirement accounts (IRAs) worth millions.

Many people disparage IRAs because the maximum annual contribution amount is currently limited to $2,000 per person — and there are lots of restrictions. If you have children who are teenagers or are in their 20s with earned income, persuade them to open Roth IRAs and/or to convert their traditional IRAs to Roth IRAs if their adjusted gross income (AGI) is less than $100,000. When they elect to take distributions 40 to 50 years later from their Roth IRAs, they won't have to pay any income tax on any of the tax-deferred growth.

There is considerable confusion about the types of IRAs (Simple, SEP, Education, Traditional and Roth) and about their specific rules involving contributions, transfers and withdrawals. This chapter provides answers to 38 questions about IRAs.

219

When were IRAs started?

In 1974, the Pension Reform Act created individual retirement accounts (IRAs) to benefit people who were not covered under a pension or by the government. Since 1981, Congress has extended IRA eligibility to include anyone with earned income (with certain income restrictions on deductibility as well as to non-working spouses).

220

I am a widower with a $500,000 IRA that lists my five children as equal beneficiaries. My financial consultant suggested that I divide my IRA into five equal and separate accounts so that each child may be named as sole beneficiary of one account. Do you agree?

Your financial consultant's suggestion is sound. By separating your IRAs for each beneficiary, you maximize the deferral period for each beneficiary. If you left your IRA with five beneficiaries, your required minimum distributions will be calculated based on the joint life expectancy of your oldest beneficiary and you. Separate accounts for each beneficiary must be established prior to the death of the IRA holder and before age 70-1/2. For example, if your oldest child was 50 and youngest was 30, the required minimum annual distribution following your death would vary for your oldest from 1/33.1 of $100,000 ($3,021) to 1/52.2 of $100,000 ($1,916) for your youngest. In fact, the IRA for the youngest could remain in effect for more than 50 years.

221

Can I transfer securities from my investment account into my SEP for my annual contribution?

No, you can only contribute cash or money funds to a simplified employee pension plan (SEP) or IRA. However, you can transfer or roll securities from an existing retirement account into a SEP or IRA.

222

Would distributions from a variable annuity within a Roth IRA be taxable?

No, distributions from a Roth IRA are tax-free regardless of the investments within it.

223

When I file my income taxes next year, do I have to inform the IRS about the Roth IRA I opened this year?

No, you're not required to file IRS Form 8606 (Nondeductible IRAs for Roth IRAs). You are only required to file Form 8606 when you make a non-deductible contribution to a traditional IRA or convert it to a Roth IRA. The form gets attached to your tax return.

224

I filed for an extension on my income taxes until August. Can I make my IRA and Keogh contributions then?

You can postpone your Keogh contribution until August but the deadline for your IRA contribution was April 15, of the year your taxes were due.

225

Must contributions to a SEP-IRA be made by April 15th (or the Monday after) like an IRA?

No, contributions must be made by tax filing date PLUS extensions.

226

I converted my traditional IRA to a Roth IRA in 1998 and am paying the tax over four years. If I were to die within this four-year period, would my wife have to pay all these conversion taxes in one lump sum?

No, you would owe remaining amounts due to the conversion included on your final return. Exception: A spousal beneficiary may continue the deferral of the conversion income over the remainder of this four-year period. Your wife could absorb your Roth IRA into her own Roth IRA and may continue to benefit from the four-year rule for paying these conversion taxes.

227

Is it worth contributing $2,000 to both my IRA and my wife's IRA if we don't touch it until we are 65? Both of us are 37.

Yes, I believe it is worth contributing to both IRAs. Each of you would contribute $2,000 annually for 28 years (a total outlay of $56,000 each, $112,000 combined). If we assume you invest in growth mutual funds averaging 12 percent annual returns, you would have an additional $381,398 each ($762,796 combined) at age 65 to better enjoy retirement. If you don't touch these funds until you are 70-1/2 (the age when mandatory distributions begin), the combined amount, $762,796, would have increased to $1,424,965 — and it only cost you $112,000 out-of-pocket.

228

Can I borrow from my IRA?

No. If you borrow from your IRA, the distribution amounts' tax-deferred status is nullified, and therefore is subject to ordinary income taxes (plus a 10 percent premature distribution penalty if you're under age 59-1/2 or unless you're disabled).

229

Can I use part or all of my IRA as security for a loan?

No, the IRS considers using any money from an IRA as security for a loan to be a prohibited transaction. The amount you use will be treated as a distribution and you will have to add that amount to your gross income for income tax purposes. If you are younger than 59-1/2, you may also be subjected to a 10 percent premature distribution penalty tax.

230

Are retirement plans such as my SEP-IRA protected from creditors?

Under the Employment Retirement Security Act of 1974 (ERISA), defined benefit (pension plans) and defined contribution plans are protected from creditors during bankruptcy. SEP-IRAs and IRAs are not protected from creditors during bankruptcy under ERISA. Some states offer protection to IRA and SEP-IRA holders from creditors. You need to consult with a competent bankruptcy attorney in your state. How do you find one? Look for a *board-certified* bankruptcy attorney.

231

Are IRAs exempt from seizure under state and federal laws?

Yes and no; it depends upon the laws of each individual state. However, IRAs are not exempt from IRS liens.

232

How much is the allowable contribution per year for someone with more than one IRA?

IRA contributions are limited to a maximum of $2,000 annually per person regardless of the number of IRA accounts. Non-working spouses are also permitted to contribute $2,000 annually to one or more IRA accounts.

233

My spouse died recently and listed me as the beneficiary for the IRA account and I rolled it into my existing IRA account. Am I permitted to subsequently roll it to a qualified retirement plan?

No, once funds from an IRA rollover are commingled with contributed funds from another plan, subsequent rollbacks are not permitted. Suggestion: to avoid commingling of IRA funds, establish separate IRA accounts. There is no limit on number of IRA accounts allowed or on number of beneficiaries.

234

What are the IRA rules for a QDRO?

A QDRO (Qualified Domestic Relations Order) normally divides an existing IRA in two parts — one for each spouse. It allows an IRA to be distributed to a spouse without being considered taxable or premature if it is rolled over into an IRA account within 60 days even if the recipient is younger than 59-1/2 years old. A distribution by reason of a QDRO may not be rolled over to another qualified retirement plan.

235

I noticed that my IRA is marked single life expectancy. What difference does this make?

A single life expectancy designation may be a big mistake! It forces you to take a larger required minimum distribution and have an increased tax burden when you start to receive mandatory distributions after age 70-1/2. Under this arrangement, your non-spouse beneficiaries are required to take a lump-sum distribution subject to ordinary income taxes on the full amount in the year following your death, which may push them into a much higher tax bracket. You are required to use a single life expectancy if you name a charity, revocable trust or your estate as your IRA beneficiary. It is almost always better to use a joint life expectancy. A joint life expectancy, however, will allow the non-spouse beneficiaries to take distributions over their lifetimes. A spousal beneficiary is permitted to rollover the inherited IRA and start a new schedule regardless if you are using single or joint life expectancy.

Suggestion: Check with your IRA custodian (bank, brokerage

firm, mutual fund, insurance company, credit union, etc.) to ensure your IRA has a joint life expectancy. If you have already started taking mandatory distributions, it is too late to change it.

236

I did a Roth IRA conversion and discovered my adjusted gross income exceeded $100,000 because of mutual fund capital gains last year. Can I undo this conversion because my income exceeded the allowable limit?

Undoing a Roth conversion is permitted if done before the due date of the tax return for the year of this conversion. This undoing process of a Roth IRA conversion is called recharacterization.

237

Is an IRA considered community property?

There are currently nine community property states; Arizona, California, Idaho, Louisiana, Nevada, New Mexico, Texas, Washington and Wisconsin. Your IRA may be considered community property if you live or have ever lived in one of these nine community property states. Please check with an attorney from the community property state.

238

Several years ago I delivered a baby that subsequently turned out to have cerebral palsy. Now, along with others, the hospital and I had been named in a suit that has been dragging on for almost five years. I am in my 70s and retired, and I wonder if my pension and IRA can be seized if there is a judgment against me.

I am not an attorney and am not permitted to give legal advice. Under the Employment Security Retirement Security Act (ERISA), pension plans are exempt from seizure by creditors under this federal law. I suggest you check with your local creditors rights attorney and ask if IRAs in your state are protected from seizure by creditors. Federal law does not protect IRAs, SEPs, and Simple IRAs since they are not considered qualified plans. Even though IRAs may be protected from seizure by selected state laws, courts (judges and juries) have recommended seizure in past cases.

239

I am married, and employed in a setting where I have maxed out my 403b plan (no private practice). My annual income fluctuates between $85,000 and $120,000. Am I eligible to contribute to Roth IRA for myself and my wife who is not working?

Absolutely, as long as your joint adjusted gross income (AGI) is less than $150,000, you and your wife are eligible to contribute up to $2000 each to a Roth IRA.

240

What taxes are owed (capital gains vs. ordinary income tax) for stocks traded in traditional versus a Roth IRA?

You owe no capital gains or ordinary income taxes on transactions within your IRA; traditional or Roth IRA. IRAs are tax deferred and you will owe ordinary income taxes when you take normal distributions from your traditional (not from your Roth) IRA except on that portion that represents after-tax contributions.

241

If I make nondeductible IRA contributions using after-tax money, and then take distributions in 20 to 30 years, what is to prevent the IRS from taxing these contributions twice?

You, the taxpayer, are responsible for filing IRS Form 8606 for nondeductible IRA contributions. You are also responsible for substantiating or providing documentation when receiving distributions from your nondeductible contributions. Otherwise you may be taxed twice.

242

I will be 70-1/2 this year and the required minimum distribution (RMD) from my IRA Rollover account is about $125,000. Do you recommend I pay it this year or delay paying it until next year?

If you delay taking your initial mandatory distribution until April 1 of the year after you reach age 70-1/2, you will be required to have two distributions that year. This double distribution in one year will probably boost your income to a higher tax bracket, and cause you to pay additional income taxes. The IRS penalty for not taking the required minimum distribution is 50 percent of the amount left that you did not take. If you only took $100,000 instead of the $125,000 RMD, leaving $25,000 short, the penalty would be $12,500.

243

I am 73 years old and wish to transfer my IRA to another custodian. May I take my required minimum distribution after my IRA is transferred?

No, if an IRA is transferred or rolled over after the account holders reach age 70-1/2 or older, the required minimum distribution (RMD) for that year will be accelerated. You must take the RMD before transferring your account or leave an amount equal to it in the existing account if you do not wish to receive your distribution early.

244

I started receiving a non-penalty distribution from my IRA under substantially equal payments provision when I was 56 years old. May I stop receiving distributions when I become 59-1/2?

No, you are required to take payments at least annually until you are 59-1/2 or for five years, whichever period is greater. Since you were age 56 when you began receiving payments, you must continue taking annual payments until age 61.

245

If I want to receive a distribution from my Roth IRA when I am 50, is there a penalty?

Yes, if you receive a distribution before you reach age 59-1/2 from your traditional IRA or the earnings of your Roth IRA, you will be subject to a 10 percent penalty and ordinary income tax. The amount of your contributions to a Roth IRA is not subject to the penalty or ordinary income tax since you used after-tax money. When taking premature distributions from your Roth IRA, your after-tax contributions are considered by the IRS to be withdrawn before the earnings of these contributions. There is no penalty until you exceed your cost basis or after-tax contributions.

246

What are the tax consequences of placing an IRA in a revocable trust?

You will accelerate income and this will create a complete distribution subjecting the entire proceeds to ordinary income tax rates plus 10 percent penalty if you are younger than 59.

247

Am I eligible to contribute to a Roth IRA if I'm participating in my employer-sponsored retirement plan? My joint income is $140,000 before taxes.

Yes, you and your spouse are each eligible to contribute $2,000 to Roth IRAs as long as your adjusted gross income (AGI) is $150,000 or less. Your participation in your employer's plan does not affect your eligibility to contribute to a Roth IRA. Contributions to a Roth IRA are not tax deductible, and the earnings may be withdrawn tax-free upon reaching age 59 — and after five years. You are not required to take minimum distributions at age 70.

Special note: non-working spouses have the same eligibility rules as working spouses.

248

Can I move my 401(k) plan (which has 11 investment choices) from a previous employer to an IRA with my broker — and suffer no tax penalties? Any advantages to moving it?

Yes, you may move your 401(k) into an IRA without any penalty. You'll have a lot more investment choices in a IRA account with a brokerage firm, and you won't have to deal with your former employer about your funds. You will also be in full control of your retirement funds and have literally thousands of investment choices — rather than only 11.

249

If my new husband made a new will leaving everything to me, but did not change his IRA beneficiary (who is still his former wife), would I inherit his IRA when he dies?

No. The beneficiary designation in a retirement plan supersedes a will. As long as his former wife is the beneficiary, she will get the money in his IRA.

250

In order to convert a regular IRA into a Roth IRA, I must have an annual adjusted gross income of less than $100,000. My income is $93,000 but my IRA amount is $60,000. Won't the IRA conversion of $60,000 cause my adjusted gross income to go up by $60,000 to $153,000 — and make me ineligible for a Roth IRA conversion?

No. The Roth conversion amount ($60,000) is not added to your adjusted gross income (or AGI) ($93,000) for qualification purposes. You are eligible for conversion to a Roth IRA because your AGI remains $93,000. For tax purposes, $60,000 is added to your AGI.

251

Do you recommend placing IRAs in a revocable trust?

No, because placing an IRA in a revocable trust would have tax consequences for the entire amount of the IRA. Please check with your tax adviser for information about your specific situation.

252

My timing was wrong! I converted my regular IRA into a Roth IRA, when the market was at its highest. Since then, the value of my account has dropped more than 20 percent in less than three months. But I may be in luck: isn't the amount of tax I owe based upon the value of my account at time I converted it?

Good news! You're right that the amount of tax you owe on your Roth IRA is based upon the value of your account at the time of time of the conversion. The IRS made a technical correction to the Taxpayers Relief Act of 1997. This correction permits taxpayers to undo their Roth IRA conversions and return the money to a regular IRA before the income tax due date for the year of the IRA conversion. Beginning in the year 2000, you have to wait until the later of January 1, 2001 or 30 days after the recharacterization to put the money back into the Roth IRA.

253

Can I roll over my 401(k) retirement plan into a Roth IRA?

Yes, you can if your adjusted gross income is $100,000 or less. But you can't roll your 401(k) directly into a Roth IRA. First, you need to roll your 401(k) over into a traditional IRA, and then convert that new IRA into a Roth. Once you've converted to a Roth, you'll owe income tax on the amount you've converted. If you converted to a Roth in 1998, you are permitted to pay the tax in four equal installments.

Caution: If your income is close to the $100,000 mark and you're considering converting to a Roth, capital gains on mutual funds you own (which may be considerable) could boost your adjusted gross income above the $100,000 mark.

254

When my 28-year-old son asked me if he would be better off investing in his 401(k) plan or in a Roth IRA, I wasn't sure what to tell him. What would you advise?

Advise your son to invest first in his 401(k) — especially up to the point his employer matches or partially matches his contribution.

255

Am I eligible to contribute to both an IRA and a 401(k) plan?

Yes. Contributions to your 401(k) plan are deductible; however, your IRA contribution may not be deductible if your income is above the limitation. If you make a non-deductible IRA contribution, make sure you file IRS Form 8606. This will prevent you or your beneficiary from having to pay taxes on the amount of your non-deductible IRA contribution.

256

How popular are IRAs? Roth IRAs?

According to Investment Company Institute (ICI), 39 percent of U.S. households owned at least one type of IRA in 1999. Ownership by type was Traditional IRA: 25 percent, Simple & Sep IRA: eight percent, Roth IRA: seven percent and Education IRA: three percent. There is some duplication because ownership of more than one type of IRA is permitted.

Chapter 6
Reducing Taxes

Many investors are only concerned with the return they receive on their investments, instead of on their real rate of return. They are shortchanging themselves, because taxes and inflation reduce their real rate of return. By using tax-deferred vehicles such as retirement accounts and annuities, these investments will not be reduced by annual income taxes and will compound faster. Properly structuring and titling your investments and timing your deductions and gains advantageously may minimize taxes.

257

What suggestions for making it easier and cheaper for my accountant to prepare my income taxes?

Many accountants send their clients tax preparation worksheets or client organizers to complete in advance of the first client meeting. Complete this worksheet accurately and legibly. I asked my accountant for suggestions she would share with you. She commented that many clients forget to include all reportable taxable events and then must file amendments and pay penalties when omissions are realized. She recommends that clients send her copies of closing statements for real estate transactions as they occur during the year so that they may be placed in the client's file ready for the next tax season. Other documents to send your accountant are receipts for major purchases. Another suggestion was not to summarize your categories such as capital gains because if you make an error in the summary, tracking it will waste a lot of time and cost you extra. Instead cross check your documents such as Form 1099 for each security you own. Since you are probably being charged an hourly fee, you'll save if you organize your records and receipts by category and separate them neatly in labeled folders.

258

Can I avoid paying capital gains taxes by selling my mutual funds before a capital gain is paid?

Yes. I suggest you call your mutual fund company to learn when and what your capital gains distribution will be.

259

I just received a 1099 for capital gains on a mutual fund I own, and the market value was down for the calendar year. Is there a way to avoid having to pay taxes on mutual funds that lose money?

This phenomenon, known as "phantom income," occurs when a fund showing a loss for the year still distributes a 1099. Here are some solutions. Purchase mutual funds with low turnover or purchase funds in a variable annuity. (Before last year, stock mutual fund investors had less of a problem paying capital gains because their funds had appreciated substantially.)

260

What can I do with an old computer that I no longer use?

Many of us have replaced our what-we-thought were state-of-the-art personal computers when we bought them with less expensive computers that are faster and have longer memories. Since we have no use for the old computer, why not find it a more appreciative home?

Many charitable organizations/schools do not have money to buy computers to do basic functions like word processing, and could use old computers that are in working condition. Before donating yours, check with your accountant about getting a charitable deduction for your computer's fair market value. You might say, "it's not worth much!" but the tax deduction will be more than you're currently getting and you free up the space it occupies. For those of us buying new computers, if we wait two years we'll probably get a comparable computer with twice the capacity and speed at half the price. These are some of the benefits of technological progress.

261

I am an immigrating physician who has been in the United States for three years. Once my status as an immigrant is established, I plan to sell my overseas residence. Will I get any tax benefit when I bring in money to buy a house in the United States?

No, you get no tax benefit by importing money to the United States to purchase a primary residence.

262

Does it ever make sense for a married person to file a separate rather than a joint tax return?

Yes, normally it is better to file jointly since the combined tax you have to pay is lower when you do. But not always. Here's an example. Let's assume that the husband has lower income and also has very high medical expenses (representing less than 7-1/2 percent of their joint incomes but significantly more than 7-1/2 percent of his income). In this case, it would probably make sense to file separately and be able to deduct his medical savings above 7-1/2 percent of his adjusted gross income. I suggest you check with an accountant to determine which filing method is more beneficial for your individual situation.

263

What states do not have a state income tax?

Right now, seven states do not tax income. They are: Washington, Florida, Texas, South Dakota, Nevada, Alaska, and Wyoming.

264

In your recent Answerman column about states having no income tax, you forgot one: New Hampshire.

New Hampshire does not have a tax on earned income. However there is a five percent tax applied to interest and dividend income over $1200 for a single person and $2400 for a married couple filing a joint New Hampshire tax return.

265

You mentioned seven states currently without a state income tax. My wife and I reside in one more, Tennessee.

You are correct that Tennessee has no state income tax on earned income but there is a six percent income tax on dividends and interest.

266

Do you think the flat tax as proposed by Steve Forbes, when he was running for President, will be adopted in the near future?

No, I think opposition from special interest groups will prevent it from being adopted in the foreseeable future. I believe Forbes' legacy will be informing Americans of the need to simplify our complicated tax code.

267

What is the "kiddie tax"?

To discourage high tax bracket parents from gifting income producing assets to the low tax bracket children under age 14, Congress passed the "kiddie tax" and indexed it for 1998. Unearned income over $1400 of children younger than 14 is taxed at their parent's tax bracket. There is no tax due for the first $700 of the child's unearned income, and the next $700 is taxed at the lowest bracket, 15 percent.

268

I am planning to lease a car soon. Can I deduct the lease price from my tax return? Is there any difference regarding taxes between buying and leasing a car?

Let's assume you use the car 50 percent for business (based upon mileage driven excluding normal commuting mileage to and from work). You can deduct 50 percent of your lease payments if you can substantiate the mileage with a daily log. If you purchase a car, you cannot deduct your purchase price, but you may deduct the portion for business use based upon a depreciation schedule. You may also deduct applicable expenses including insurance, gas, oil and maintenance. Please consult a CPA before deciding to lease or purchase a car.

269

Our family has a limited partnership. I have two sons starting medical school next year. We would like to loan each of them some money from the partnership. I understand I will need to use the Applicable Federal Rates to set the interest rate for the loans. Can we defer the interest payments for the time they are in school? And are there any other rules I should know in setting up the loans?

You are dealing with a delicate issue — loaning money to your own children and allowing them to not pay interest on these loans for the current tax year. Please check with a competent attorney (preferably the one who set up your family limited partnership) or your CPA to advise how this can be done without the IRS claiming this was not a loan but a gift tax event.

270

I am about to join a local practice and become their third partner. I have heard that there were places that offer to repay loans in an attempt to recruit physicians, but I do not know how they have fared. I would like to know if it is possible to have my medical student loans repaid by the company? If so, if there would be any benefits for the company? Or even if the company paid it off for me and it was allotted to my portion of the company's expenses, could this be done before taxes?

I am not qualified to answer your questions and have asked Steven Peltz, an experienced medical practice specialist and consultant to physicians, to answer it. His response: Educational loans, as any other loans are deductible to the extent of the interest. If the geographic area qualifies under a special federal program, the federal government may participate in paying back the loan. The practice's accountant should be the first source of ideas and review for suggestions such as if the practice pays off the loan on a pre-tax basis and then charge it to you as income, it may cost less than if you received your salary after taxes and then wrote out a personal check. The interest on the loan, which is not deductible to you, may be through the practice. Your compensation could then be adjusted based on the amount of interest paid by the practice for you on a pre tax basis. The practice may also make the decision to pay off a portion of the loan and call it a recruiting expense. Or the practice may lower your salary by an agreed upon amount and pay off the loan in one year.

Steven Speltz has offered to answer any questions. You and readers may call him at 914-277-4070 or email him at speltz@docsbackoffice.com .

Chapter 7
Paying for College

My elder daughter graduated from the University of Pennsylvania 35 years after I did. The cost of my education for four years was less than the cost of her education for one semester. My younger daughter graduated from Columbia two years later, and her education cost considerably more than her sister's.

There are many types of educational funding plans available today, such as state prepaid college tuition plans, Education IRAs, and the College Savings Plans Network. In addition, IRS Section 529 plans permit individual to make annual gifts in excess of $10,000 — without using any gift or unified estate tax credits. Questions about these plans are answered in this chapter.

A growing number of Americans are in the "sandwich generation." They are sandwiched between paying college bills, funding retirement plans and even providing support for elderly family members. Although it can represent a financial challenge to fund a child's education, most people realize the importance of doing so: Studies have shown that a college education can boost lifetime income by more than $1 million.

271

What is an education IRA? Who can set up and contribute to an education IRA?

An education IRA is an IRA established to pay the qualified higher education expenses for any child under age 18. Anyone can contribute up to $500 cash each year for an education IRA whose modified adjusted gross income is not more than $110,000 or $160,000 if filing a joint return.

272

Are contributions to an education IRA deductible?

No, they are not deductible. Earnings on an education IRA grow tax free until they are withdrawn.

273

Can both sets of grandparents open and contribute $500 to an education IRA for the same child?

No, the annual contribution limit is $500 per child, regardless of the number of contributors.

274

Can money in an education IRA be invested in life insurance?

No.

275

If we set up an education IRA for my son and he does not go to college, do we have to pay income tax on the growth?

Not if the education IRA is rolled over to another education IRA to benefit other members of your family. Eligible family members include other children, stepchildren, grandchildren, parents, grandparents, nephews, nieces, and in-laws.

276

Can a student waive the tax-free treatment of an education IRA withdrawal and elect to pay any tax owed on this withdrawal?

Yes, the student or his parents may then be eligible to claim a tax credit (Hope or Lifetime Learning credit) for higher education expenses paid in that tax year. By waiver of the tax-free treatment of the education IRA and taking the credit, taxpayers may actually reduce the amount of taxes due.

277

What is the difference between prepaid tuition and college saving plan programs?

Prepaid tuition plans lock in the cost of college at today's prices. Grandparents, parents, and other interested parties make lump sum contributions or monthly installment payments to prepay tuition at any of a state's eligible colleges or universities. College savings programs permit participants to invest monies in a special college savings account.

278

Can I contribute to a prepaid tuition program and also an Education IRA for my child?

No, not in the same tax year.

279

Where can I get information on these plans?

Nineteen states offer prepaid tuition plans and 27 states offer college savings programs. The following chart lists these states and the telephone numbers to call for additional information. The College Savings Plans Network (CSPN) of the National Association of State Treasurers provided this information. For more information, please visit their website at www.collegesavings.org or call toll-free at 877-277-6496.

COLLEGE SAVINGS PLANS NETWORK
08/02/00 2:37 PM
State College Savings Plans Overview
(*Italics* represent no residency requirements)

STATE	NAME OF PROGRAM	DATE OPER.	TYPE	PHONE #
Alabama	Prepaid Affordable College Tuition	✔1990	Prepaid Tuition	800-252-7228
Alaska	Advance Coll. Tuition Pmnt. Program	✔1991	Prepaid Tuition	800-478-0003(*)
	Alaska Savings Plan	Dec-00	Savings Plan	907-474-5927
Arizona	Family College Savings Program	✔June-99	Savings Plan	602-229-2592
Arkansas	GIFT College Investing Plan	✔Dec-99	Savings Plan	888-442-6553
California	*Golden State ScholarShare Trust*	✔Oct-99	Savings Plan	877-728-433
Colorado	*Colorado Prepaid Tuition Fund*	✔Sept-97	Prepaid Tuition	800-478-5651
	Colorado Savings Plan	✔Oct-99	Savings Plan	
Connecticut	*Connecticut Higher Education Trust*	✔Dec-97	Savings Plan	888-799-2438
Delaware	*Delaware College Investment Plan*	✔July-1998	Savings Plan	800-292-7935
Florida	Florida Prepaid College Program	✔1988	Prepaid Tuition	800-552-4723
	Florida College Savings Program	2001	Savings Plan	850-488-8514
Georgia	HOPE Scholarship		Scholarship	800-776-6878
Hawaii	Hawaii College Savings Program	2000	Savings Plan	808-586-1518
Idaho	*Idaho College Savings Program*	2000	Savings Plan	208-334-3200
Illinois	College Illinois!	✔Oct-98	Prepaid Tuition	877-877-3724
	Illinois College Savings Pool	✔Mar-2000	Savings Plan	217-782-1319
Indiana	*Family College Savings Program*	✔1997	Savings Plan	888-814-6800
Iowa	*College Savings Iowa*	✔Sept-1998	Savings Plan	888-446-6696
Kansas	*Postsecondary Education Plan*	July 2000	Savings Plan	785-296-3171
Kentucky	Education Savings Plan Trust	✔1990	Savings Plan	877-598-7878
	Guaranteed Pre-Paid Col. Tuition Plan	Aug-2001	Prepaid Tuition	502-564-4722
Louisiana	Louisiana START	✔July-9	Savings Plan	800-259-5626, ext. 0523
Maine	*Maine College Savings Program*	✔Aug-99	Savings Plan	877-668-1116
	Maine Prepaid Tuition Program	2000	Prepaid Tuition	877-668-1116
Maryland	Maryland Prepaid College Trust	✔Apr-1998	Prepaid Tuition	888-463-4723
	Maryland Savings Plan	2001	Savings	888-463-4723
Mass.	U.Plan	✔1995	Prepaid Plan	800-449-6332
	U.Fund	✔Mar-1999	Savings Plan	800-544-2776
Michigan	Michigan Education Trust	✔1988	Prepaid Tuition	800-638-4543
	Michigan Education Savings Program	TBA	Savings	800-638-4543
Minnesota	Minnesota EDVEST	2000	Savings Plan	800-657-3866 ext. 3201

STATE	NAME OF PROGRAM	DATE OPER.	TYPE	PHONE #
Mississippi	Prepaid Affordable College Tuition	✔1997	Prepaid Tuition	800-987-4450
	Mississippi Affordable College Savings	Fall 2000	Savings	800-987-4450
Missouri	*Family Higher Education Savings Plan*	✔Nov-99	Savings Plan	888-414-6678
Montana	*Family Education Savings Program*	✔1998	Savings Plan	800-888-2723
Nebraska	Nebraska College Savings Plan	2000	Savings Plan	402-471-2455
Nevada	Prepaid Coll. Tuition Plan Trust Fund	✔Oct-98	Prepaid Tuition	888-477-2667
New Hampshire	*Unique College Investing Plan*	✔July-98	Savings Plan	800-544-1722
New Jersey	Better Educational Savings Trust	✔Aug-98	Savings Plan	877-465-2378
New Mexico	Name Pending	TBA	Prepaid Tuition	800-279-9777
New York	*College Choice Tuition Savings Prog.*	✔Sept-1998	Savings Plan	877-697-2837
N. Carolina	College Vision Fund	✔June-1998	Savings Plan	800-600-3453
N. Dakota	*ND Higher Education Savings Plan*	2000	Savings Plan	800-472-2166
Ohio	Ohio Prepaid Tuition Program	✔1989	Prepaid Tuition	800-233-6734
	College Savings Program	Fall 2000	Savings Plan	800-233-6734
Oklahoma	Oklahoma College Savings Plan	✔Apr-2000	Savings Plan	405-858-4422
Oregon	Oregon Qualified Tuition Savings Prog.	Jan-2001	Savings Plan	503-378-4329
Pennsylvania	Guaranteed Savings Program	✔1993	Savings Plan	800-440-4000
	Investment Savings Program	2000	Savings Plan	800-440-4000
Rhode Island	*RI Higher Education Savings Trust*	✔Sept 24, 98	Savings Plan	877-474-4378
S. Carolina	SC Tuition Prepayment Program	✔Sept 98	Prepaid Tuition	888-772-4723
South Dakota	No program			
Tennessee	Tennessee BEST	✔1997	Prepaid Tuition	888-486-2378
	Investment Savings Program	✔2000	Savings Plan	888-486-2378
Texas	Texas Tomorrow Fund	✔1996	Prepaid Tuition	800-445-4723
Utah	*Educational Savings Plan Trust*	✔1996	Savings Plan	800-418-2551
Vermont	Vt. Higher Education Savings Plan	✔Dec-1999	Savings Plan	800-642-3177
Virginia	Prepaid Education Program	✔1996	Prepaid Tuition	888-567-0540
	Virginia Education Savings Trust	✔Dec-99	Savings Plan	888-567-0540
Washington	Guaranteed Education Tuition Program	✔Summer-98	Prepaid Tuition	877-438-8848
West Virginia	WV Prepaid College Plan	✔Oct 98	Prepaid Tuition	800-307-4701
	WV Investors Program	2000	Savings Plan	800-307-4701 ext. 2
Wisconsin	*EDVEST Wisconsin*	✔1997	Savings	888-338-3789
Wyoming	Advanced Payment for Higher Education Cost	✔1987-95	Prepaid Tuition (a)	307-766-5766
	Family College Savings Program	✔May 2000	Savings Plan	307-777-7408
Dist. of Columbia	National Capitol College Savings Trust being proposed to DC Council			

KEY:
TBD — To be determined
Italicize — no residency requirements
(*)   —Toll free available for in-state calls only
✔   — Program operational

NOTES:
(a) Program suspended in 1995 because of non-participation, but counted as active because it is honoring previous contracts.

SOURCE: The College Savings Plans Network of the National Association of State Treasurers.

"THE NUMBERS"

Current Prepaid
19 (Alabama, Alaska, Colorado, Florida, Illinois, Maryland, Massachusetts, Michigan, Mississippi, Nevada, Ohio, Pennsylvania, South Carolina, Tennessee, Texas, Virginia, Washington, West Virginia, Wyoming)
Note: Wyoming program suspended.

Prepaid To Be Operational
3 (Kentucky, Maine, New Mexico)

Current Savings
27 (Arizona, Arkansas, California, Colorado, Connecticut, Delaware, Illinois, Indiana, Iowa, Kentucky, Louisiana, Maine, Massachusetts, Missouri, Montana, New Hampshire, New Jersey, New York, North Carolina, Oklahoma, Rhode Island, Tennessee, Utah, Vermont, Virginia, Wisconsin, Wyoming)

Savings To Be Operational
14 (Alaska, Florida, Hawaii, Idaho, Kansas, Maryland, Minnesota, Mississippi, Nebraska, North Dakota, Ohio, Oregon, Pennsylvania, West Virginia)

Legislation Pending for Savings
1 (Michigan)

Long Range Total:
Prepaid=22 Savings=42 Total = **64**
Representing 48 states

For more information, visit the CSPN web site at http://www.collegesavings.org
Or call toll-free 1-877-CSPN496 (277-6496)

280

We are invested in a state prepaid college tuition program for the benefit of our son. Will there be a tax on the difference between the amount we initially invested and the amount it has grown into?

Yes. Your son will receive a 1099 annually for this difference from the college when he attends. This amount is reported to the IRS and uses the student's Social Security number.

281

What if my son does not attend college after we have set up an Education IRA and made annual contributions?

You may elect to rollover these funds to an Education IRA of another family member without having to pay tax.

282

It seems that the new tax law changes regarding deductible student loan interest specifically exclude most physicians. Does the phase-out period really end at an AGI (adjusted gross income) of $55,000? If I qualify by making a low enough salary, may I deduct interest on loans older than 60 months if they are refinanced?

The maximum student loan annual interest deduction is $2,000 for year 2000, and $2,500 for year 2001 and later years — provided your modified adjusted gross income is $40,000 or less (single filer) or $60,000 or less (joint filer). The amount of the deduction is phased out as your modified adjusted income increases to $55,000 ($75,000 in the case of a joint return). You cannot deduct interest on loans older than 60 months even if they are refinanced. The 60-month limitation is based upon the original loan date. For additional information, you can get IRS publication 970: "Tax Benefits for Higher Education."

283

Can I really give more than $20,000 annually to my grandson's education fund without having to pay gift taxes under the College Savings Plan?

Yes, under a separate provision of IRS Section 529 plans, you can invest as much as $50,000 ($100,000 for married couples) per beneficiary in one year without being subject to gift taxes. Contributions made in one year may be prorated over a five-year period without incurring gift taxes.

Under Section 529 plans, neither your unified estate nor gift tax credit is reduced as long as you make no more gifts to that beneficiary during the five-year period and live five years. Let's also assume you and your spouse wish to establish an education fund for your six grandchildren and also want to reduce your estate tax liability. By setting up a 529 college savings plan for each grandchild with $100,000, you have immediately removed $600,000 from your taxable estate without using any of your gift or unified estate tax credits.

Chapter 8
Understanding Estate Planning

Frequently, *Physician's MONEY DIGEST* conducts an online survey and physicians answer anonymously. Recently, the survey topic was "Do you have a will?" Overall, it's estimated that two-thirds of all American adults do not have wills. I was surprised to learn that it's the same for physicians: two-thirds of physicians responding to the online survey did not have wills.

What happens when you die without a will? This forces the state or courts to appoint guardians for your minor children and decide who will receive your assets after your death. Well, your spouse will be guardian of the children. What happens if he or she also dies?

By preparing a will, you ensure that your personal goals are met for the disposition of your assets. Peace of mind is your immediate reward.

For those with significant assets, I use the following

image to demonstrate how crucial it is to have a will. I ask participants to close their eyes and visualize a number flashing on a screen. This number is their total net worth, including the face value of any life insurance they own. Then, I ask them to imagine the Dow Jones Industrial Average dropping 4,000 points in one day! I ask them to picture their revised net worth flashing on their imaginary screen. I tell them to open their eyes and explain that one day dramatic drop on the Dow and their net worth is comparable to the effect of estate taxes on what they will leave to their loved ones. Federal estate tax rates go as high as 55 percent!

This chapter contains answers to 15 questions from physicians concerned about estate planning. The previous chapters dealt with wealth creation; this chapter on estate planning discusses wealth preservation. The estate tax is a voluntary tax; it is avoidable with proper lifetime planning. Think of estate planning as wealth transfer planning and take a proactive approach so that you control the disposition of your assets.

284

What is meant by estate equalization to reduce taxes?

Estate equalization is a restructuring strategy for combined estates of married couples exceeding double the applicable exclusion amount ($675,000 in 2001 and will gradually increase to $1,000,000 by 2006). By taking advantage of the exclusion amount of $675,000 in each estate, a couple is able to exclude $1,350,000 ($675,000 X 2) from federal estate taxes.

285

I am a 68 year old retired physician and my spouse is 66. We live in a small Southern city and our four adult children are self-sufficient. Each child is happily married and has children. Our oldest daughter has a very successful medical practice. Our net worth is about $3.6 million; almost 1/2 in my IRA that I do not really need for living expenses. Our lifestyle is modest and we have no debts. We have wills leaving everything equally to our four children and do not as yet have long term care insurance. Since I am going to be required to start taking money out of my IRA in two years, do you recommend I start early?

Your IRA is a ticking time bomb from a tax standpoint. Between estate and income taxes, 70 percent+ of your IRA may go to the IRS and not to your family. I suggest you and your spouse meet with a competent estate-planning attorney licensed in your state and discuss the following topics:

1. Start taking distributions from your IRA so that you can pay premiums for a second to-die life

insurance policy for you and your spouse. Have the attorney establish an irrevocable life insurance trust (also called a wealth replacement trust) to own this $1 million policy. Your beneficiaries will receive 100 percent of the death benefit without having to pay income tax or estate tax on the insurance proceeds.

2. Set up revocable living trusts for both of you. Assets in trusts are not subject to probate administration and avoid attorney and executor's fees. This is also referred to as an AB Credit Shelter trust and permits the uniformed credit for both of you to be used.

3. Inquire about how to fund your revocable living trusts. The trust must be the legal owner of the assets to avoid probate administration, provide supervision of assets for minor or incompetent children and reduce death taxes. If title to your assets has not been properly transferred in the name of the trust, they are not part of the trust and subject to probate.

4. Discuss the possibility of excluding those of your children who wish to turn down an inheritance from you to avoid estate taxes when they pass it on to their children. If your child is financially well off, does not want or need the money, and prefers that you designate their children (your grandchildren) as heirs then one layer of estate taxes may be eliminated.

5. Explore long term care insurance as a form of

portfolio insurance in case you and your spouse need it. One out of two people will require long term care during their lifetime. You need to be insurable to qualify for this insurance.

286

Will my estate be subject to probate twice? I own real estate in a neighboring state and have a will.

Yes, real estate owned in other states not held in trust may also be subject to probate in the state in which it is located.

287

Should I own life insurance policies on my own life?

Life insurance owned in your name may increase your estate tax liability. The proceeds or the death benefit are added to the value of an estate if it is owned by the insured. Estates in excess of $675,000 in 2001 begin to be taxed at 37 percent of the value. So, for example, if a $675,000 estate has to add proceeds from a $500,000 life insurance policy, the estate tax would be $185,000. However, if this policy were not owned by the insured but placed in an irrevocable life insurance trust, there would not be any estate tax due.

288

I am an 83-year-old internist practicing medicine part time. I have no children and wish to establish a school for blind children in my will. The value of my estate is $1,500,000. Any suggestions?

I recommend that you meet with a board-certified estate-planning attorney in your area and learn the best ways to make sure your wishes are fulfilled. Discuss the benefits of a charitable remainder annuity trust with your attorney. If it is structured properly, you can enjoy a significant tax deduction while you are alive by transferring highly appreciated assets to a charitable remainder trust without having to pay any capital gains tax. The trust will pay you a six to seven percent annual income for the rest of your life and revert to your designated charity after you die.

289

My financial advisor convinced me to meet with a board certified estate planning attorney because my net worth is $5.3 million ($2 million in a retirement plan) and we have wills. I am 63, my wife is 60 and we started with nothing and don't want to set up elaborate trusts for our four adult children and six grandchildren. We refuse to spend $40,000 for annual premium for a second-to-die life insurance policy to be put in an irrevocable trust. After all, our children will inherit a lot more than we did. Any comments?

It is your money and you have the right to make the IRS rather than your family, the major beneficiaries of your estate. By not establishing and funding simple credit shelter trusts, you or your wife will waste your federal Unified Estate Tax Credit. You are allowed to pass the first $675,000 of assets in 2001, to $1,000,000 in 2006, to your beneficiaries free of estate and gift taxes. Your estates are tentatively in the 55 percent federal tax bracket (over $3,000,000). By establishing the life insurance trust to replace the money spent on your estate tax and income taxes (your retirement plan), your family will inherit $2,800,000 more which will not be subject to federal estate or income taxes.

290

Any comments on estate planning? What are the pros and cons of creating a trust?

According to *The Tools & Techniques of Estate Planning* by Limberg, "every estate is planned — either by you or by the state and federal governments." Many Americans are uncomfortable dealing with estate planning issues because they have to confront their own death. When discussing this issue with clients, they frequently refer to this matter by saying, "if I die" rather than "when I die." Even though death is a certainty, many are reluctant to do estate planning, hoping the issue can be postponed indefinitely. *Business Week,* January 8, 1996, estimated that seven out of 10 Americans die without a will. The one relative whom they think is least suited to raise their minor children may be awarded custody by the court. Why? The parents never specified otherwise in a will or trust and the court did not know their wishes.

291

My wife and I own a vacation home in a different state than the one our primary residence is in. Recently I inherited my parent's home, which is in a third state. Since we own property in three states, can we select the most favorable state for our estates to be probated?

Sorry; each state may wish to hold probate proceedings and your estates may be subjected to three separate and costly probate proceedings. I recommend that you consult with an estate-planning attorney where you have your primary residence.

292

When must federal estate taxes be paid?

The Internal Revenue Code requires that federal taxes be paid in within nine months of the date of death. There are provisions to permit the executor an extension to pay these taxes from a decedent's business if the IRS believes there is a reasonable cause to grant an extension. Suggestion: consult a CPA before requesting an extension.

293

What percent of estates pay estate taxes?

According to the IRS, only one to two percent of estates are greater than the exclusion amounts and are required to file federal estate taxes.

294

I am an American citizen married to a non-citizen. I'm trying to convince my wife of the substantial tax benefits of her becoming a citizen. If she does, it will eliminate the need for her to pay estate taxes if I die first. We have a $2.5 million estate. Any suggestions?

Is she willing to pay $833,000 not to become a citizen? Because that's what it boils down to, tax-wise. Let's say she remains a non-citizen and you were to die first. Based on the size of your estate, she would then owe $833,000 in federal estate taxes (assuming that you have a simple will). That's nearly a third of her inheritance. Instead, let's say she becomes a U.S. citizen. Since there is an unlimited marital deduction for U.S. citizens, then if you were to die first she would owe no federal estate taxes on her inheritance. I suggest both of you visit a competent estate planning attorney who can also explain how you may be able to greatly reduce and possibly eliminate estate tax upon the death of the remaining spouse.

295

As the executor and only beneficiary of my Dad's estate, I know that I am entitled to a fee as executor. Doesn't it make sense to take this fee since this amount would be paid from the estate and not be subject to federal estate taxes?

Yes, you are correct about an executor's fees being a deductible expense to your father's estate and reducing exposure to possible estate taxes by the amount of your fee. However, the fee would be taxable as ordinary income to you. *Suggestion:* Have your accountant compare your personal income tax rate with your father's federal estate rate so that you can choose the strategy with the smaller tax.

296

A physician is sued for malpractice and dies before the judgment is rendered. The plaintiff subsequently wins an amount greater than the insurance coverage limits. Can the plaintiff collect from the physician's estate? Are the spouse's assets part of the physician's estate and subject to seizure? Would a living trust of the spouse be helpful in protecting these assets? Also, if the spouse receives death benefits from a life insurance policy on the physician, are these proceeds also attachable by the judgment?

I contacted Jeff Kahn, a board-certified estate planning attorney and CPA, for advice about your questions since I am not an attorney. Jeff is also a CFP estate-planning instructor. He commented that whatever is in the physician's probate estate will be subject to creditor's claims. He felt a living trust would probably help to shield the wife's estate assets since the trust is private (unlike a will, which becomes a matter of public record). If this physician transferred his assets after the suit was filed with the intention of denying access to his potential creditors, then this transfer could be invalidated based upon applicable state laws.

Benefits paid to a designated life insurance beneficiary are not attachable by creditors. If you or others wish to communicate directly with Jeff Kahn, his telephone number is 954-757-6100 and his email address is jkahn@attorney-cpa.com.

297

My wife is a physician with two offices in a major city. I manage her offices. We are both 53 years old, and we have four children — two in medical school and two in high school. Our assets are liquid (investments = $1.1 million, IRAs = $275,000, home = $300,000 and each of us has life insurance for $500,000). Do we need estate planning? How much will it cost? What will we save by doing it?

If you establish revocable living trusts for you and your wife and then retitle your assets so that they are in the trusts, your estates will be able to shelter $1,350,000 instead of $675,000 in 2001. This $1,350,000 you'll both be able to shelter from estate taxes will gradually increase to $2,000,000 in 2006. Federal Estate tax rates begin at 38 percent and go up to 55 percent. What will you save? By having two trusts established and funded properly, the additional $675,000 that is not subject to 38 percent will save $247,000 in federal estate taxes. It will cost about one to two percent the amount of the savings to establish trusts by a competent estate-planning attorney. You would not go to a real estate or divorce attorney for estate planning. By planning your estate now, you and your wife can ensure that your assets are properly titled and distributed with minimal estate taxes to your loved ones.

298

My wife and I are Canadians and are planning to apply for U.S. citizenship after the five-year waiting period. What estate tax exemption do we qualify for now as non-U.S. citizens? Does the unlimited spousal transfer at death apply or is the exemption capped at $60,000 (v. $600,000 for U.S. citizens)? Most of our assets are held jointly. I am aware of Qualified Marital Domestic Trusts (QDOTs) but given the legal costs to establish a QDOT, wouldn't I be better off just increasing my life insurance coverage for the next two years?

At the time this book goes to press, non-U.S. citizens only qualify for a $100,000 estate tax exemption; U.S. citizens qualify for a $675,000 estate tax exemption in 2001. This exemption will gradually increase to $1,000,000 by 2006. The unlimited spousal transfer applies only to surviving spouses who are U.S. citizens, unless the inherited assets are sheltered in a Qualified Marital Domestic Trust. If the term insurance premiums are significantly less than the costs for setting up this trust and you are insurable, insurance may be the cost-effective choice. Please consult an estate-planning attorney before you decide.

Chapter 9
Insurance / Home Ownership

Physicians need disability insurance to protect their earning power. And they need long-term-care insurance to protect their assets from being depleted to pay nursing care costs for themselves or an elderly parent.

I strongly recommend that anyone buying or selling a home use a qualified real estate attorney even if it costs 1/2 of one percent more. Why? It's a rule of thumb I have: Do what you do best and hire the rest. I have heard horror stories about people closing on a home without an attorney. Later there were problems with clear title and small-unresolved issues became very costly for the legally unrepresented party.

299

I am a 35-year-old self-employed internist. My mutual fund investments have averaged 20 percent+ yearly returns for the last three years. I'm considering increasing my investment in these funds by increasing my home mortgage to 125 percent of market value. The net return after mortgage payments would be almost 10 percent. Do you think this would be too risky?

Yes. If the income from your medical practice drops and you are unable to pay the increased mortgage payments, you risk losing your home to foreclosure. Remember, the returns you've been getting for past three years are not the historical norm and past performance is no guarantee of future results. The stock market returned an average of 11 percent annually over the past 74 years, according to Ibbotson Associates — not 20 percent+. I do not believe the extra benefit or return you are trying to get justifies the risk of losing your home.

300

Do you recommend Medicare supplement or Medigap policies?

Medicare supplement policies and Medigap policies are the same. Commercial insurers and Blue Cross and Blue Shield organizations developed these policies to close the gaps between the cost of medical care for people over 65 and reimbursement under Medicare. There are ten levels of coverage for Medicare supplement policies designated by letters A through J. The National Association of Insurance Commissioners sets standards. Plan J has the most comprehensive benefits and Plan A has the most limited benefits. All applicants for Medigap must be accepted when they apply for coverage within six months after they enroll in Medicare after age 65 regardless of pre-existing health conditions. For a free Guide to Health Insurance for People with Medicare, please call 1-800-638-6833 for this comprehensive 50-page booklet. This booklet was prepared jointly by the National Association of Insurance Commissioners and the Health Care Financing Administration of the U.S. Dept. of Health and Human Services.

301

Is mortgage insurance on a home necessary?

Think of mortgage insurance as life insurance on the mortgagee or the person who is the income producer for the loan. In case of that person's death, the surviving family may not be in a position to make the payments. Mortgage insurance covers those payments so that the surviving family may continue living in the home — ideally, free of mortgage payments. Frequently, mortgage insurance policies have a decreasing term, which spans the life of the loan.

302

My parents are retired public school teachers in their mid 60s and have modest financial resources. I am the only child who is financially able to help if there is a medical crisis requiring expensive nursing home care. Do you suggest I purchase long-term care insurance for them?

Yes, if your parents are insurable, it makes a lot of sense. The Alzheimer's Association estimated that one in 10 Americans 65 and older have Alzheimer's disease; it goes up to almost 50 percent at age 85 and older. They also reported that the approximate average lifetime cost per Alzheimer's Disease patient is $174,000. It is the third most expensive disease after heart disease and cancer.

Since almost half of Americans will require home health or nursing home care in their lifetimes, a good long-term care insurance policy can be an excellent investment. We know that the health problems of one parent tend to adversely affect the health of the care-giving spouse. Most retirees want comfort, dignity and independence. By providing sound financial planning for your parents in case of a medical crisis, you have helped to assure their comfort, dignity and independence.

303

I am employed as an attending physician in a major hospital and want to start a clinic at home to see patients in the evening. If this clinic is successful, I'll expand its hours and work only part time at the hospital. If not, I plan to relocate within two years. Should I buy property or rent it?

I recommend that you rent rather than buy, since real estate can be an illiquid investment. You may not be able to sell it if and when you wish to relocate. I suggest that you try to rent with an option to buy so that you have more flexibility.

304

I am considering refinancing my home mortgage. Do you think the Federal Reserve will raise interest rates this year?

Trying to predict the Federal Reserve's actions is an exercise in futility because there are too many domestic and international economic and political variables.

305

When does it make sense to refinance my mortgage?

Most people refinance their mortgages to reduce their monthly payments and/or to cash out if their home has built up equity. Your credit history will affect the interest rate the bank quotes you. The rule of thumb for refinancing used to go something like this: If the interest rate on a new mortgage is two or more percentage points less than the existing mortgage, then it makes sense to refinance.

Nowadays, more people use the following formula (if your objective is to reduce your monthly payments): If your total refinance costs can be made up in 18 months or less, then refinancing makes sense. (The formula is: Total cost of refinancing divided by monthly difference equals number of months to break even with refinancing.)

> For example:
> Total cost refinancing: $4,250.00
> Monthly difference in payment: .... $ 255.00

You'll be ahead by refinancing beginning in the 17th month. Go ahead and refinance.

306

Five years ago, I purchased a convertible term insurance policy when my twin daughters were born. Because I was still in residency, we bought annual renewable term insurance to get maximum protection at the lowest cost. Even though I was treated successfully for cancer last year, I am uninsurable. Do you recommend that I convert my term insurance policy into a regular life insurance because a physical is not needed. In addition, won't my term insurance premiums eventually become cost-prohibitive?

Yes. If there are no health qualifications to convert from term to universal life, it makes sense to get this coverage you normally would be denied. The initial premiums will be considerably greater than term premiums, because you'll be building up cash value and be guaranteeing coverage that will remain in force for the rest of your life. Eventually, when your twins are past college age and you don't need this coverage to protect your family, you may wish to consider placing this insurance in an irrevocable trust. This will reduce the size of your estate and will make your children and/or grandchildren your beneficiaries.

307

How are accelerated death benefits under a life insurance policy determined?

Many life insurance policies are now offering "accelerated death" benefits to insured individuals who have a life expectancy of six months or less. If a terminally ill insured person has a life expectancy of more than six months but less than two years and needs money for medical or other reasons, then accelerated death benefits (sometimes called a "viatical agreement") may be a good solution. Here's how it works. Under this kind of an agreement, the insured person sells his/her life insurance policy to an individual or organization. The accelerated death benefits received are tax-free to the insured person. Depending upon the insured person's life expectancy, he or she will generally receive 60-90 percent of the face value of the policy. If a policyholder's current policy permits accelerated death benefits; he/she will probably receive a higher percentage of the face value than if he/she used an outside company.

308

I was refused a mortgage because of an unfavorable credit report. I have always paid my bills on time and thought my credit was perfect. When I read my credit report, I learned they thought I was someone in another state with the same name who was a credit card deadbeat. What can I do to prevent this from happening?

I deeply sympathize with you for having to go through this nightmare. I recommend that everyone periodically orders a copy of his or her credit report to check its accuracy with a national credit reporting agency. If you find any errors, let the agency know in writing via registered mail (return receipt requested).

309

I have a property in Vermont. When we were building a home there, we discovered toxic waste on ten acres. I received a settlement from the company that dumped it (to make up for the loss in value to my property after the state put deed restrictions on it). How do I handle this come tax time? I was told this was an "involuntary conversion." And my accountant in California can't answer any of my questions. I'm hoping you can.

I am not a CPA, but I called the IRS Hotline for help (1-800-829-1040). According to IRS Publication 17, the settlement income you received should be reported on Schedule D as "no gain" or "no loss." It is considered a non-taxable event.

310

I will be selling my home about four weeks after I close on the purchase of a new home. What do you think of borrowing or cashing in my IRA to pay for the purchase, and then depositing the proceeds from the sale back into the IRA within 60 days to avoid paying tax and 10 percent penalty?

You're right about being able to use the 60-day IRA rollover provision once a year — as long as you redeposit the funds in the same or another IRA account within 60 days. However, I can not recommend using your IRA as a "swing" or "bridge" loan to finance the purchase of your new home. Here's why. If the buyer of your old home runs into a problem that delays the closing past 60 days or if he/she backs out of the deal, you're in trouble. Not only would you have to pay taxes and a 10 percent penalty, you would not be permitted to redeposit these funds and would lose the future tax deferred benefits of your IRA.

311

My son and I inherited a $200,000 home overseas when my husband died almost two years ago. We plan to sell this home this year. Will the money from this sale be subject to US taxes?

U.S. citizens are subject to capital gains taxes regardless of the location of the assets they sell. However, the value of the home inherited is valued for tax purposes at time of death. For example, if the value of the home at the time of your husband's death was $200,000, and it was later sold for $200,000, there is no gain and therefore no U.S. capital gains tax due.

312

I am a 44-year-old single male physician with two school-aged children in a rural area. I choose to work part time since I am a Mr. Mom and my annual income is $85,000. I contribute the maximum to my employer sponsored retirement plan and my Roth IRA. I plan to retire when I am 60. I am able to invest an additional $3000 each year and have received conflicting advice as to the better place to invest this money. Both my friend and my accountant suggest investing in a tax-sheltered annuity. My conservative investment advisor, who is also a very good friend, told me that if I invest in good growth mutual fund and paid the taxes each year, I'd be better off at age 60. Who is right? And why?

You'll be better off at age 60 if you invest now in a variable annuity because it grows within a tax shelter. Tax-deferred investing compounds more than taxable investing that is reduced by annual taxes.

313

Are dividends paid on insurance policies taxable?

No. Dividends paid on insurance policies (participating policies) are not considered taxable income. They are considered a partial return of the insurance premiums you've already paid. Dividends are usually used to purchase additional insurance benefits, or may be applied as a discount to an existing premium. If you are no longer insurable, you still may be able to get additional coverage by using your dividends to purchase it.

314

My wife and I originally purchased our home for $255,000 in 1968 and it is presently worth $1,100,000. If we sold our home and purchased a new one in a retirement community, how much would we have to spend to eliminate capital gains tax on the sale?

Under the current tax law, you and your wife each are exempt from paying capital gains taxes on $250,000 in gains on the sale of your home. You alluded to the rollover rule permitting the deferral of capital gains tax for homeowners purchasing a home of equal or greater value than the one they sold. This was repealed by the Taxpayers Relief Act of 1997. Let's assume you and your wife sell your home for $1,100,000 and your cost basis is $350,000 (original purchase price plus costs of improvements such as new roof, etc and selling expenses). Your capital gains would be $750,000 and your capital gains tax due would be calculated as follows:

$1,100,000 - $350,000 (cost basis) = $750,000
$ 750,000 - $500,000 (exemption amounts) = $250,000
$ 250,000 X 20 percent capital gains tax rate = $50,000
tax due

Before selling your home, please consult with your accountant and be represented at both closings by a real estate attorney.

315

Do you recommend using qualified or non-qualified monies to purchase long term care insurance?

If your premiums are paid with after tax dollars (non-qualified), then any benefits you receive will not be taxable. If your premiums are paid with income that has been withheld and not as yet been subject to taxes (qualified), then any benefits you receive will be subject to taxes (ordinary income). This rule on taxing of long term care insurance benefits also applies to the taxing of disability benefits.

316

I am a 41-year-old physician currently in the midst of a general liability lawsuit alleging breach of confidentiality. The hospital's insurance company is covering the defense but will not pay if the judgment is for the plaintiff. The insurance company will try to get me to pay. I am currently renting and would like to purchase a home, which would be co-owned by my father and me. Would this be safe if the judgment is against me? Also is my pension safe?

Please realize the attorney from the insurance company is not working for you but for the insurance company. However you definitely need to have someone in your corner representing and protecting your interests. Hire a competent attorney so that the insurance company knows they can not steamroll you and abandon its responsibilities. Your defined benefit plans such as pension plans, 401(k) plan are protected from creditors by federal laws (ERISA). Suggest you consult with your local attorney about buying a home jointly with your father since state laws vary about homestead protection.

317

We are going on a three-week trip to Europe and wonder what is a good Travel Health Insurance?

Most Europeans and Canadians buy travel insurance when traveling abroad so that they have health insurance coverage. Americans buy primarily trip cancellation insurance and not health insurance. Many Americans are not aware that their health insurance or health plan will not cover them when they leave the U.S. Also, Medicare does not provide coverage outside the U.S. There are comprehensive travel insurance programs that include medical insurance, trip cancellation, emergency evacuation and additional benefits.

Chapter 10
Personal and Family Matters

Have you ever seen a Brinks truck follow a hearse to a cemetery? Probably not. Yet some people place more importance on money than any other aspect of their lives — as if they could take their money with them. Physicians have told me that some of their wealthy patients with terminal illnesses would surrender their wealth for good health. Others have said that what really matters most are the relationships you have with your family and friends.

Our final chapter consists of 15 questions from physicians about personal and family matters. They're followed by an interview with Sundeep Bahn, CEO, and Greg Scott, CFO, Medsite.com, online support for physicians.

318

I am 63 and considering marrying someone I have known since we were together in high school. Both of us have adult children and grandchildren from prior marriages and we are financially secure. Do you recommend a prenuptial agreement?

Yes, I recommend both of you visit competent attorneys specializing in marital and family law not real estate law or general practice. A prenuptial agreement becomes a necessity for later term marriages because of the need to protect extended families. Realize that prenuptial agreements should be reviewed every two to three years and may be amended. Frequently an absence of this agreement leads to wills being contested under the justification that one spouse used undue influence on the other.

319

I am a retired doctor, and my wife has no interest in understanding our investments. Any suggestions for arranging our finances so that my wife will receive a steady monthly income if I become incapacitated or die before her?

It sounds as if you want your investments to run on automatic pilot so that your wife does not have to make any decisions or changes. One good solution might be to create a portfolio of quality diversified mutual funds, and then arrange for your wife to receive a systematic monthly withdrawal. The total amount withdrawn each year should be six to eight percent of your original investment.

In addition, if you and your financial adviser pick the right blend of stock funds, plus (for some people) some good balanced mutual funds, your nest egg will be protected against inflation.

Balanced funds may be useful because they've been returning 10–11 percent a year for the past 30 years. If this historic return continues, then even if your wife's withdrawals total 8 percent a year, your balanced funds would still make money.

Balanced funds, incidentally, usually buy a mixture of common and preferred stock, plus bonds. The idea here is to get income *and* enough growth to protect your nest egg from being cracked by inflation.

320

My wife and I are in our late 30s and have separate successful medical practices in a small Midwestern city. We met in medical school and have three children, ages six, four, and one. We are not spenders; we save and invest about 30 percent of our combined incomes. Right now, we're disagreeing over my choice of a car. I have a 10-year-old compact car that has high mileage, but runs okay. I use it only for my daily commute — eight miles each way. My wife wants me to buy a new car (not a compact) and I think it's a waste of money. Do you think it makes financial sense for me to continue driving my existing car or to spend money on a new car?

Normally, I avoid taking sides in disagreements between spouses. But in this case, I think your wife is 100 percent correct. If you were to be involved in a serious automobile accident in a compact car (rather than in a newer and larger car with more and better safety features), your risk of being maimed, disabled or killed is much greater. I realize you only use your compact for a short commute. However, if two cars only going 30 m.p.h. meet in a head-on collision, the impact is comparable to a 60 m.p.h. crash. Why expose your wife and children to an increased risk of not having a husband or father?

Several months ago, one of my Florida clients was driving north to Washington, DC, on an interstate with his wife. A sizable rock must have fallen off of a truck in front of them and was going to hit the windshield on the passenger's side. While swerving to the left to avoid the rock, the car rolled over and the air bags deployed. The car was totaled, but my clients were not severely injured. As they were being driven by the tow truck operator, they were told how "fortunate they were driving a car with a strong roll bar which prevented the top from crushing them when their car rolled over." The tow truck operator also mentioned that, in his experience, only Mercedes, Volvos, Saabs and BMWs are equipped with an extra-strong rollbar. Financially, you are a money machine and will earn millions of dollars during your career. I believe that whatever you do to protect your earning power makes sense financially. Go buy a new car with all the safety features including side airbags and let your astute wife help select it!

321

My brother, sister and I contribute equally to supporting our elderly father. May we each claim him as a dependent?

No. Since none of you contributes more than 50 percent to your father's support, none of you is eligible to claim him as a dependent. Suggestion: if two of you sign a multiple support agreement, the third sibling can claim your father as a dependent. To be fair, rotate each year so that every three years each of you will be eligible to claim your father as a dependent.

322

My teenage nephew was recently a victim of a severe bus accident, and has become permanently disabled. My sister, his mother, was advised to see an attorney to set up a special needs trust. What is a special needs trust? And do you recommend we set one up?

A special needs trust is normally established by parents with disabled children who are receiving state or federal assistance, such as supplemental Social Security benefits (SSI). This trust allows the parents to provide some monetary help to their children without disqualifying them from continued public assistance. Property held in a special needs trust does not usually count as a resource of the disabled person if access to this trust is restricted. I recommend consulting a trust attorney who is very experienced in setting up special needs trusts.

323

Would you recommend that the winners of a $30 million lottery take a reduced lump sum amount or payments spread over 20 years?

I would recommend the immediate lump sum. There is no tax advantage to take a reduced amount over time since both options would be taxed at the maximum rate of 39.6 percent. Hopefully, the winners would hire a professional team of investment, income and estate tax advisors to help them maximize the risk-adjusted return and lower the amount reduced by federal and state income and estate taxes.

324

I have been a practicing internist for the last three years and my fiancé is a surgeon. He wants us to get a prenuptial agreement so that his assets will be protected in case I am sued — and vice versa. After we get married, if he were to die suddenly, would his five-year-old son from a prior marriage automatically get all the assets/properties he acquired before our marriage? Would everything then be under the control of his ex-wife since she would become their son's legal guardian?

You need to consult a matrimonial attorney in the state where you live who specializes in QTIP Trusts (Qualified Terminable Interest Property Trusts) and prenuptial agreements. That attorney should only represent you and not your fiancé. Make sure all your what-ifs are answered.

325

I have a terminal illness and realize I made a mistake of not involving my wife in any of our financial matters. We have no children and I have handled the finances completely during our 32 years of marriage — everything from making the investment decisions to writing checks to pay our bills. What do you recommend I do within the next year to prepare her to cope financially without me?

In many families, I have found that one spouse has assumed primary responsibility for the family's money matters. If that spouse dies first, the surviving spouse may have a hard time handling personal financial matters along with settling a spouse's estate. Frequently the wife was the one responsible for handling the finances while her husband pursued his career.

I recommend that you involve your wife in family finances by immediately placing her in charge under your loving guidance. Teach her to reconcile the checkbook balance with the bank statement balance, set up a filing system for your finances by category, pay bills before the due date, and prepare a manual of your family finances so that she feels comfortable with it. Show her your monthly cash flow on an annual basis so that she understands what the monthly income and expenditures will be after you are gone.

You will need to update your records and get rid of outdated files. Prepare a statement of net worth listing all assets and liabilities as well as the location of any documents, certificates of ownership, deeds, insurance policies, wills and trusts. You and your wife need to meet with your professional advisors — your accountant, your financial advisor and your attorney — and have an open discussion with them of what kind of guidance and advice she can expect to receive from them.

Your wife needs to feel comfortable with these advisors — not intimidated by them.

326

I am a 32-year-old emergency care physician who graduated from residency two years ago. **My girl friend is an internist. We are building our first home this summer and we're wondering if there are any legal considerations we've overlooked.**

If either one of you were involved in a fatal car accident, the surviving partner would not get 100 percent ownership rights to the home. Without a written agreement, the deceased's estate would own 50 percent of the home. The surviving partner may not have the available funds to purchase his former partner's share. If the partners had not entered into an ownership agreement as joint tenants with rights of survivorship, the home may have to be sold to pay the claims of the deceased's estate. Other reasons for having a legal agreement between you and your girl friend include disability, claims from creditors and the possibility that one or both decides to split up. Since you are investing in the construction of a new home, I suggest that you spend a little extra for a competent attorney to prepare the legal documents to protect both of you from the "what-ifs."

327

I am a 43-year-old physician and my wife has an executive position with our state government. We live in a small town and have three children. Our combined income is $200,000 but we have no savings because my wife (who has tendencies to shop compulsively) and I went through an expensive divorce from each other. We recently remarried after being divorced two years. I'm concerned that we may have money problems again but she assures me that it won't happen. What do you suggest?

You need to know your current financial state so that you have a starting point. I recommend you order individual credit reports to learn what credit agencies are saying about both of you and correct any inaccuracies. These credit reports will also show credit cards and charge accounts in your names. Eliminate as many credit cards as possible. Do this by cutting them in half and returning them with a letter that asks the issuer to cancel your account and to send you an acknowledgement. I suggest you send it via registered mail (return receipt requested). If you have eliminated all your credit card debt, you will no longer pay interest charges. You and your wife may need counseling to learn to budget, live within your budget, and start to invest your savings by paying yourselves first. Investment plans are needed for college funding for your children and your retirements. I suggest you also use a competent financial planner who will act as a financial coach to help both of you achieve your goals together. This coach will be able to view your situation more objectively and unemotionally than you can.

328

What is the difference between titling property my wife and I own as "joint tenants with right of survivorship" or "tenants by the entirety?"

Joint tenants with right of survivorship (JTWROS) permits two people to own property together as co-owners. When one co-owner dies, the surviving co-owner automatically receives both interests. JTWROS may be used by married couples and unrelated people. Neither owner may sell or refinance without the permission of the other. Creditors of one owner can force the sale of a property to satisfy a judgement even though the co-owner did not benefit from the debt.

Unlike JTWROS, tenants by the entirety prohibit a creditor from forcing the sale of the asset to satisfy debts of a co-owner. Tenants by the entirety are only allowed for legally married couples.

329

My son has about $10,000 of debt. Mostly car loans, college debt, and credit card balances. He is going to live in a house I recently bought and he will only be paying utilities and upkeep (minor). He has about $15,000 of equity in his present dwelling. I have advised him to sell it, pay off his debt and start to accumulate equity in other investments. He insists on renting this property as he feels he will get some income and the property will increase in value, therefore he will make more money that way. I think it is a big mistake, but sons don't always listen to their fathers. Please give me an impartial opinion that I can show, even if you don't totally agree with me.

It would be better for your son to get out of debt and invest in more liquid investments especially those that are tax-deferred. Does your son participate in his employer's retirement plan? You mentioned that your son does not pay his credit card bills in full each month and probably has to pay 18 percent+ interest charges? Does your son have an IRA? A Roth IRA?

Win-Win Suggestion: Offer your son an incentive to put away money in his retirement plan by matching him 50-50. For every dollar he personally invests, you will put up one dollar. Good luck to both of you!

330

My sister was a widow. When she died, her three adult children argued constantly with each other over her estate. Now they hardly speak to each other. I very much want to make sure that this doesn't happen to my family. Any ideas on how to do that?

No matter how old you are, the death of your last parent is one of the most emotionally wrenching times anyone can endure. Many brothers and sisters whose relationships were harmonious until then find themselves arguing bitterly over their parent's assets. Those arguments have been known to permanently and painfully damage those relationships.

To avoid the kind of pitched battles you fear, talk to a competent estate-planning lawyer — and share your concerns with him or her. You can prevent a lot of arguments by specifying in your will who gets each valuable asset you own, be it a piece of jewelry, a work of art, stocks, bonds, or anything else. If your will spells out who gets what, then your heirs won't have any questions about what you wanted. But don't let what you're doing take them by surprise after you've died. Bring this delicate issue out in the open. Talk to your children in a friendly family meeting so they'll know what your wishes are. That way, they can understand why you're doing what you're doing.

331

I'm a recent widow. I don't understand the statements I get in the mail about my mutual funds from my broker. Any suggestions?

Yes. I suggest you keep separate files for each of your accounts to hold confirmations and correspondence. It's a good idea to place your statements in a loose-leaf binder divided by statement period (month or quarter). When you read your statement, compare the account value for the current period and the prior period. Usually the elements of a statement include the cash and money funds balance, which show purchases and sales of securities; deposits, interest or dividends received and withdrawals or checks written.

The portfolio details section shows the value of your holdings on a specific date. And the transaction details section gives you a chronological summary of all activity within this period. I suggest you ask your broker or his/her sales assistant to explain how to read your statement. If your statement indicates a check was mailed to you or a security was delivered and you did not receive it, notify the local branch manager of the missing item. When you send a check payment for a security, your check should be made payable to the firm with your account number on the front of the check. Your check should not be made payable to an employee of the firm.

332

I am an internist, aged 57, and handle the finances for our family. My wife, aged 53, has no interest in learning about our personal finances. This concerns me because I know if I were killed in an accident tomorrow, she would not be prepared to manage the family finances. What do you recommend?

According to the Census Bureau, American females outlive American males by approximately seven years. Women generally marry men three to seven years older. For Americans aged 65 and older in 1997, 46 percent of the women were widows and 16 percent of the men were widowers. I recommend you show this column to your wife so that she understands her financial security may depend on her ability to manage the family finances if something should happen to you. I suggest that she accompany you whenever you meet with your professional advisors — your accountant, your estate-planning attorney and your financial advisor. It is vital that she feels comfortable with these professionals and they explain recommendations so that she understands them. As a financial consultant, I generally will not meet with prospective clients unless both spouses are present.

Interview with CEO & CFO Medsite.com

Medsite.com is a leading Internet provider of services to the medical community. Beginning with its first venture, MedBookstore.com, Medsite has rapidly expanded to include electronic physician credentialing, online medical supplies (such as stethoscopes and specialty instruments), and continuing medical education (CME) online. Four University of Pennsylvania graduates with entrepreneurial inclinations and talents started Medsite in 1997. Their success was heralded in a recent PENN alumni publication and caught my attention. The following is my conversation with CEO Sundeep Bhan and CFO Greg Scott.

333

What percentage of physicians do you think are on the Internet?

Bhan: The numbers right now range anywhere from 60 to 70 per cent.

More important, however, is the number of physicians using the Internet for their medical professional needs. We have about 250,000 registered users; about 200,000 of them are medical professionals and students and the figures are growing every day.

Scott: Part of our strategy is to meet doctors at very early stages of their professional careers. We cater to students and residents, mostly through our bookstore offerings. Most of these younger professionals are very web-savvy. I think that by catering to physician's needs right now that are not directly related to the practice, we can introduce physicians to the web.

334

What trends do you see in the health care industry today? Are physicians faced with continued financial pressures from third-party payers?

Bhan: The first trend we've seen in the health care industry has been movement on the IT (information technology) side. A lot of companies came out with back office connectivity solutions (these solutions automate routine administration tasks in a physician's office) — for claims processing, EDI transactions (electronic data interchange), billing and practice management.

The second big recent trend has been companies going directly after consumers like Dr.Koop.com. The next wave we are beginning to see is a stronger focus on the physician. It's good to empower the physician where you have the connectivity back office solution already in place for the doctor's practice. Now you are going out and educating and empowering the consumer which is great — but let's not leave the physician out of the picture. So our strategy is to empower the physician and to provide the right tools to allow patients and physicians to interact with each other.

Scott: Physicians also need to be business people. In any business, there are continued pressures on income and on the need to find new ways to make their practices more efficient. So there will always be pressures on reimbursement — whether it's from third-party payers or from individuals as we move into different types of care down the road. So the income pressures will always be there. Our strategy is to help physicians cope with those income pressures, so they can better manage their practices. This way, they increase the time that they spend with their patients, and reduce the time needed to deal with administrative tasks like ordering supplies or dealing with claims, or eligibility problems.

335

What percentage of medical books are purchased online? What savings incentives are there for medical students to purchase from you?

Bhan: We started selling software with clinical applications on CD-ROM about five years ago, through distributors, at more than 200 stores. We discovered that the distribution infrastructure for getting products such as medical books and software to our customers — physicians — was cumbersome. So we started selling on the Internet — before amazon.com and e-commerce. We did it by putting our phone number out there. People would call us directly and order software from our Internet site. That was how the idea for creating e-commerce applications for professionals came about. In the fall of '97, we began leveraging our relationships with our distributors to sell all the products in their warehouses through our website. People visiting our website to buy books are motivated by price, convenience, and selection. There is currently no sales tax, and we offer discounts of up to 10 percent on books.

336

How can physicians enroll in Medsite's online CME program?

Bhan: Enrolling for CME on the Internet is easy. Physicians can take the courses they want, pay by credit card and never leave their offices. There is also the CME tracker, which tracks CME credits as a convenience. We're also able to offer free CME classes at pharmaceutical companies.

337

How will Medsite Filer help physicians reduce costs and delays from third-party payers?

Scott: Medsite Filer is not specifically designed to reduce accounts receivable delays. It is a money-saving tool for physicians and for managed-care organizations. One of the great hassles for managed-care organizations is keeping all of their participating physicians fully credentialed. It is a requirement to be NCQA (National Committee for Quality Assurance) accredited that a health plan re-credentials all of its physicians every two years.

Bhan: Medsite Filer is designed to allow the physicians to eliminate costs in their own practices. It keeps all fully primary source verified credentials online for virtually instantaneous online delivery to whatever managed care organizations the physician wishes to deliver that information to. So it takes the hassle out of the credentialing process — one that has traditionally taken a lot of the paperwork and a lot of time. Medsite filer is a money-saver for managed care associations as well. It is designed to ease the credentialing process and reduce costs within a physician's office. One of the things we look at constantly is the physician's desktop, or physician's paperwork, which includes solutions we currently offer like ordering supplies, books or getting information. We also look at the online connection between the physician's office and the third-party payer.

338

Do you see e-commerce changing the way health care and pharmaceutical companies sell their products and services to physicians?

Bhan: Pharmaceutical companies spend $8 billion to $10 billion a year promoting their products and services to physicians. We offer them a focus on building one-to-one relationships with physicians. We allow for interaction between health care companies and physicians at a fraction of the traditional cost. We're always looking to find ways to create a win-win situation for everybody; we sell our products and services to physicians; physicians get products and services at a lower cost; and the pharmaceutical companies get the opportunity to better communicate with physicians.

Index
(Chapter - Question No.)

401 (k) retirement plans, 4-Intro, 4 181, 183, 185, 193, 195, investment choices 5-250, rollover to Roth IRA 5-255, comparative benefits 5-38, contribution rules 5-39
403 (b) retirement plans, 4-Intro, 4-185
accountant, assist in preparing tax return 6-257, consult prior to leasing a car 6-268
Advance-Decline Line, calculation 3-107
advice for high school students, RMarston-33
Aim, Dent Demographic Trends Fund, HDent-92
Allied Signal 3-148
alternative investments I-11
Aluminum Company of America 3-118
Alzheimer's Association, incidence 9-301
AMA, LKurtz-147
Amazon.com, market cap 2-64
American College of Radiology, GHirsch-209
American Express 3-118
American Medical Association, GHirsch-Intro
American Telephone & Telegraph 3-118
analog technology, ABarrett-168
annuity
annuity, single premium 4-190
annuity, tax code 1035 exchange 4-192
annuity, variable 4-192, reducing taxes 6-257, versus investing in mutual fund 9-311
Answerman column, HDent-Intro
asset allocation I-Intro, 3-Intro, RMarston-28
attorney, board certified estate planning - establish charitable remainder annuity trust 8-287
attorney, board certified estate planning - need to consult if non-citizen spouse 8-293
attorney, board certified estate planning - wasting federal credits 8-288, prevent conflict among heirs 10-330
automobile leasing 6-268, investing in safe car 10-319
baby boomers population, LKurtz-133

baby boomers
baby boomers, LKurtz-139
baby boomers, challenges facing them 2-55
baby boomers, spending wave 2-Intro, 2-54
baby-boomers, retiring, RMarston-27
back office connectivity solutions, Medsite-333
Bahn, Sundeep, 10-Intro, Medsite Intro
Barnes & Noble, market cap 2-63
Barrett, Andrew, 3-Intro, ABarrett-Intro
Barron's, HDent-Intro
biology, HDent-101
biotech revolution, HDent-92
biotech trends, HDent-92
biotechnology stocks, LKurtz-157
Blitzer, David 2-63
Blue Cross and Blue Shield 9-132
Boeing 3-118
bond market, European, RMarston-31
bonds
bonds, European corporate, RMarston-31
bonds, European government, RMarston-31
bonds, inflation-indexed, JSiegel-44
bonds, investing, HDent-99
bonds, US government, HDent-99
bonds, inflation indexed
Borders, market cap 2-63
Brancaccio, David, Intro-GHirsch
Bristol-Myers, LKurtz-142, 153
Britain, RMarston-17
British currency, RMarston-17
broadband, ABarrett-173, 174
budget, surplus, JSiegel-38
Buffet, Warren HDent-74, 86
business education, HDent-101
Business Week 8-289
Cable Financial News I-6
cable, companies, ABarrett-163
capital gains, JSiegel-40
career choices, RMarston-33
career planning, physicians, GHirsch-205
career selection, JSiegel-48
cash flow, during retirement 4-188
Caterpillar 3-118
CDs, callable I-10, for retirement 4-Intro

cell phone, ABarrett-160
Census Bureau 10-160, LKurtz-133
Certified Financial Planner, vs. financial planner 3-130
Chevron 3-118
CISCO, 3-122, JSiegel-37
Citigroup 3-118
Clinton healthcare plan, LKurtz-134, 147
clubs, investment I-14
CNBC-TV, HDent-Intro
CNN-TV 2-58
Coca-Cola 3-118, RMarston-16
cockroach theory 3-102
College Savings Plans Network 7-Intro, difference between prepaid tuition program, availability chart 7-279
communications revolution, JSiegel-53
community property, states 5-237, IRA 5-237
Compaq, LKurtz-157
compassion fatigue, GHirsch-208
computer illiteracy 2-64
computer manufacturers, ABarrett-177
computer science career, HDent-101
Congress, JSiegel-38
consumer sector, LKurtz-131
Crash of 1929, 2-57
credit card, debt 2-Intro, spouse is credit card junkie 10-326, 18%+ interest charges 10-328
cross-training, physicians, GHirsch-215
cross-training, nurses, GHirsch-215
currencies, consolidation, RMarston-30
currencies, three dominant, HDent-97
CUSIP number, definition 3-103
Datacom equipment growth rate, ABarrett-165
Day Trader, success rate 3-116
day-trading, RMarston-22, ABarrett-169
Deferred Compensation Plan 3-115
deficit financing 2-57
deficit, government, H-84
deflation, problems created 2-56
Dell Computer, 2-62, LKurtz-157
demographics, HDent-84, 85, 98; LKurtz-132; RMarston-27
Dent, Harry, HDent-Intro
Diamonds 3-117
digital subscriber link (DSL) ABarrett-168
disclaiming inheritance 8-284
Discovery Channel I-6
distance learning, JSiegel-46

diversification, JSiegel-52
diversification, with foreign stocks, RMarston-16
dividend yield 3-118
dividend, growth, JSiegel-40
dollar cost averaging I-1, 4-192
dollar, HDent-97
Dow 30, averages I-1, diamonds 3-117, composition 3-118, being surpassed by NASDAQ 3-122; HDent-74
Dow 36,000, JSiegel-49
Dow Jones 30, HDent-75
Dow Jones Industrial Average, JSiegel-49, HDent-74
Dr. Koop.com, Medsite-333
DSL, ABarrett-173
DuPont 3-118
duration, bond 3-119
earnings yield I-8
echo baby boom, HDent-93
Economic Influences 2-Intro
economy, HDent-80
economy, strengths, JSiegel-50
economy, vulnerability, JSiegel-51
Education IRA
Education IRA, 7-Intro, ,life insurance investment 7-274, contribution conflict with prepaid tuition program 7-277
Education IRA, definition and eligibility 7-271,272, 273, grandparent's contribution 7-273
Education IRA, rollover provision 7-275 and 7-281, waiver of tax-free treatment to preserve tax credit eligibility 7-276
Educational loans, to recruit physicians 6-270, deductible student loan interest provisions 7-282
electronic data interchange transactions, Medsite-333
Eli Lilly, LKurtz-153
Empirical Economics, RMarston-Intro
entrepreneurs, JSiegel-45
equity markets, RMarston-27
equity premium, JSiegel-44
ERISA, prohibition against seizure by creditors 4-189, created IRAs 5-219,5-239
ESPN I-6
Estate equalization 8-283

Estate Planning
Estate Planning, pros and cons 8-289, owning real estate out-of-state 8-290
Estate Planning 8-Intro, cost and need for 8-296, percent paying ,estate taxes 8-292
Estate tax, when estate taxes due 8-291, unlimited marital deduction not applicable to a non-citizen spouse 8-293
Euro, HDent-97; RMarston-26; RMarston-17
Eurobonds, definition 3-113
Europe, growth opportunities, ABarrett-162
European bond market, RMarston-31
European Union, RMarston-17
Evaluating investments, I-Intro, bond duration 3-119
Executor, fee, 8-295
expectations, unreasonable, JSiegel-35
Experion, 9-307
Exxon, 3-118
FDIC, insurance limits for CDs I-15
Federal Budget, surplus 2-58
Federal funds rate, 2-73
Federal Reserve
Federal Reserve, chairman, RMarston-25
Federal Reserve, discount rate 2-73, effect of raising interest rates 3-121, anticipating rate hikes 9-303
Federal Reserve, margin rates 2-57
financial advisor, I-9, 3-330, HDent-77, 78, 86
financial sector, LKurtz-131
fiscal policy, JSiegel-38
fixed income investment, RMarston-32
Florida 4-Intro, 4-193
Forbes, Steve, 6-266
Ford, RMarston-16
foreign stocks, 1980s, RMarston-19, 28
Fortune 100 companies, JSiegel-42
Fortune, HDent-Intro
France, unemployment rate, RMarston-18
Frankfurt Exchange, RMarston-30
French, market, RMarston-30
funds
funds, index vs. actively managed, RMarston-23
funds, leverage buyout I-11

funds, exchange I-11, I-12
funds, hedge I-11
funds, mutual-fees 3-129, source of retirement income 4-184, understanding statements 10-329
funds, oil and gas I-11
funds, private equity I-11
funds, real estate opportunity I-12
funds, venture capital I-11
Gateway Computer 2-62
GDP growth, ABarrett-166
GDP, healthcare as percentage, HDent-75
Genentech, LKurtz-142, 152, 157
General Electric 3-118
General Motors 3-118
Generation X 2-69
Generation Y 2-69
Germany, unemployment rate, RMarston-18
Glassman, James, JSiegel-49
Glaxo/Smith Kline, LKurtz-153
global economy, ABarrett-171, JS-38
Good Morning America, HDent-Intro
Goodyear Tire & Rubber 3-118
Greenspan, Alan, ABarrett-166, RMarston-25
Harris, Bretell, Sullivan & Smith-LKurtz-Intro
Harvard Medical School, GHirsch-Intro
Hassick, Kevin, JSiegel-49
Health Care Financing Administration 9-299
health insurance, non-reimbursement, LKurtz-138
healthcare
healthcare companies, LKurtz-152
healthcare dollars, LKurtz-140
healthcare expenditures, as a percentage of GDP, LKurtz-136, 137, 138
healthcare industry, HDent-75, 88
healthcare sector, LKurtz-131
healthcare system, US, LKurtz-135
healthcare systems, British, LKurtz-134
healthcare systems, Canadian, LKurtz 134
healthcare trends, Medsite-333
healthcare, investing, LKurtz-Intro
healthcare, investment prospects outside US, LKurtz-154
Hewlett-Packard 3-118,4-196,4-197
high school students, advice to, JSiegel-47

Hirsch, Gigi, GHirsch-Intro, 2-65, 66; 4-Intro
HMO, HDent-76, 77, 100 LKurtz-146, 149, 156
Holiday Effect, ABarrett-164
Home Depot 3-118
home ownership
   home ownership, refused mortgage application because of unfavorable credit report 9-307
   home ownership, protected from creditors 9-315, proper titling of ownership between unmarried couple 10-325
   home ownership, increasing mortgage to 125% of market value 9-298, need for mortgage insurance 9-300
   home ownership 9-Intro, renting with an option to buy 9-302, refinancing mortgage 9-303 and 9-304
Hong Kong market, HDent-94, 95
human genome project, LKurtz-150
Ibbotson Associates of Chicago 4-186, stock market returns past 74 years 9-298
Ice Cream Effect, on tech stocks 3-112
immigration, HDent-85
Immunex, LKurtz-157
index funds, HDent-82, RMarston-23
index funds v. actively managed funds, HDent-82
Indonesian market, HDent-94
inflation, HDent-99, JS-36
Inflation, staying ahead 2-54
insurance
   insurance, disability 9-Intro
   insurance, health while traveling overseas 9-316
   insurance, life-owned by insured 8-286, accelerated death benefits 9-306
   insurance, long term care 4-196, as portfolio insurance 8-284, pay nursing care costs 9-Intro
   insurance, paying premiums for parent's policy 9-301; funds to pay premiums 9-314
   insurance, term 8-195, converting to universal life 9-305
Intel, 3-118, LKurtz-195
intergenerational conflicts, LKurtz-141
International Business Machine 3-118

Internet
Internet companies, unprofitability, ABarrett-170
Internet sales tax, ABarrett-162
Internet stocks, mania 2-63
Internet, ABarrett-159, 160, 178; HDent-78, 80, 93, 98; JSiegel-37, 38
Internet, Medsite-Intro
Internet, revolutionizing business 2-62
Internet, stocks, HDent-96
Internet-IPOs, ABarrett-167
investing in precious metals, HDent-89
investing in real estate, HDent-89
investing, online, HDent-83
investment philosophy, stock selection, LKurtz-143
investor, home bias, RMarston-19
Investor's Business Daily, HDent-Intro
investors
   investors, biggest mistake, HDent-74
   investors, long term, JSiegel-52
   investors, mistakes, HDent-86
   investors, qualified for alternative investments I-11
involuntary conversion 9-308
IPO, pre-IPO offering I-11
IRA
   IRA, Beneficiary Designation, for multiple beneficiaries 5-220
   IRA, substantially equal payments provision 5-245, premature distribution 5-246, popularity 5-58
   IRA, year started 5-219, 1998 conversion four year rule 5-226, borrowing from and security for loan 5-229
   IRA, life expectancy designation 5-235, ex-spouse designated 5-251
   IRA, tax consequences of placing in revocable trust 5-53, Ticking tax time bomb 8-284
   IRA Distributions 4-196, 5-Intro, 5-222, QDRO rules 5-234 and 5-238, Required Minimum Distribution 5-243
   IRA, Roth IRA eligibility 5-40, Use as bridge or swing loan 9-309
   IRA, conversion to Roth IRA 3-109, 4-Intro, 4-175, seizure by creditors 4-189 and 5-239, 5-Intro, rollover 5-233

IRS Hotline 9-308
IRS Section 529 Plans, 7-Intro; explanation of reducing estate and gift tax liability 7-283
JP Morgan 3-118
January effect 2-59
Japan
   Japan, consumer sector, RMarston-20
   Japan, consumer sentiment, RMarston-20
   Japan, economy, RMarston-19,20
   Japan, stock market, RMarston-20
Japanese firms, RMarston-17
Johnson & Johnson 3-118, LKurtz-153
Joint Tenants with Right of Survivorship 10-327
Journal of Economic Literature, RMarston-Intro
Journal of International Economics, RMarston-Intro
Journal of International Money & Finance, RMarston, Intro
Kahn, Jeff, 8-295
Keogh retirement plan 4-185, 187, seizure by creditors 4-189, contribution deadline 5-224
Korean market, HDent-94, 95
Kurtz, Lloyd 3-Intro
lobbyists, healthcare, LKurtz-147
London bond market, RMarston-31
London Exchange, RMarston-30
London, financial center of Europe, RMarston-17
long-term growth prospects, LKurtz-131
long-term investing I-5, 4-192, RMarston-32
Lottery 4-181, winner select lump sum payment and use a professional team 10-322
Lynch, Peter HDent-74
malpractice suits, GHirsch-204, 208
malpractice, unpaid judgment from physician's estate 8-295
managed care, LKurtz-134, 149, 158
managing risk I-Intro
market
   market, correction I-1
   market, decline I-6
   market, swings 2-70
   market, timing I-13, 3-115
   market, volatility 2-72
Marketplace (NPR), GHirsch-Intro

Marston, Richard, 3-Intro
maximizing returns I-2
McDonald's 3-118
MDIntellinet, GHirsch-199, 200, 204
medical books, Medsite-334
medical profession, RMarston-21
medical school, RMarston-21
medical students, GHirsch-205
medical students, Medsite-334
Medicare 4-196 HDent-79; JSiegel-38; LKurtz-156; RMarston-24
medicare, reimbursements 2-61
medicine, emerging, GHirsch-182
Medigap and Medicare supplement 9-299, travel health coverage overseas 9-316
Medimmune, LKurtz-157
Medsite.com 10-Intro
Medsite.com, Medsite Intro
Merck 3-118; LKurtz-138, 153, 154
mergers, JSiegel-43
Merritt, Hawkins and Associates, GH-209
Microsoft 3-118; LKurtz-157
Minnesota Mining & Manufacturing 3-118
Mobil, 3-118
monetary policy, LKurtz-133
mortgages, floating rate, RMarston-25
multinational corporation, RMarston-16
municipal bonds
   municipal bonds, calculating tax equivalent yield 3-120
   municipal bonds, crossover definition 3-110
   municipal bonds, subject to AMT 3-111
mutual funds, RMarston-123
NASDAQ 3-Intro, 3-118, 128, RMarston-22, 30, surpassing Dow 30 3-123
National Association of Insurance Commissioners 9-299
National Association Of Investment Clubs (NAIC) I-14
Nortel, JSiegel-37
North American Security Administrators Association 3-116
nurses, cross-training, GHirsch-215
nursing home stocks, LKurtz-142
OECD Health data, LKurtz-136
online trading, ABarrett-169
P/E, information technology, ABarrett-161
Palm Pilot, ABarrett-160
patient service 2-71
paying for college 7-Intro

PBS, HDent-Intro
PC industry, LKurtz-157
PC, ABarrett-160
PEG ratio 3-124
Peltz, Steven 6-270
penny stocks 3-106
pension funds, RMarston-19
personal bankruptcy 2-Intro
Pfizer, LKurtz-138, 142, 147, 152, 153, 154
phantom income, reported on 1099 3-123, on mutual funds 6-259
pharmaceutical companies, LKurtz-148
pharmaceutical companies-estimated R&D expenditures, LKurtz-153
Pharmacia, LKurtz-153
Philip Morris 3-118
physician
   physician burnout, GHirsch-208
   physician, changing role, LKurtz-150
   physician, isolation, GHirsch-211, 213
   physician, primary-care, LKurtz-151
   physician, student loans, GHirsch-214
Physician's MONEY DIGEST, 8-Intro
physicians
   physicians, changing role, LKurtz-150
   physicians, cross-training, GHirsch-215
   physicians, declining income, RMarston-21
   physicians, financial situation, HDent-76
   physicians, HDent-86, 87, 88; RMarston-32
   physicians, profession in crisis, 2-65
   physicians, retiring early, GHirsch-209
   physicians, unions, LKurtz-158
   physicians, using Internet, Medsite-332
plastic surgery, LKurtz-139
Polaroid, RMarston-29
Pond, Jonathan 4-181
portfolio, structuring I-Intro, 4-198, systematic monthly income withdrawal 10-318
portfolio, window dressing 2-59
preferred stocks, recent drop in value 3-314
prenuptial, agreement 10-317, children from prior marriage and asset protection 10-323
prepaid college tuition program, difference between College Savings Plan Network 7-277, tax ramifications - student 7-280

Presidential election, effect on stock market 2-277
Price Earnings (P/E) I-8, 3-118
price earnings ratios, JSiegel-37, RMarston-29
Prime rate 2-73
Probate, real estate 8-285 and 8-290, guardianship issues 8-289
Proctor & Gamble 3-118
productivity, ABarrett-166
professional advice, RMarston-32
psychiatry, LKurtz-140
Quinn, Jane Bryant 3-130
real estate investments, RMarston-32
retirees 2-54, maintaining purchasing power 4-Intro, 4-180, cash flow 4-178, 10-318
retirement income, JSiegel-40
retirement plan, not yet eligible I-9, 4-Intro
retirement planning, HDent-87, RMarston-27
return on investment, real rate 6-Intro
reverse takeover, explanation 3-108
reverse-split, justification 3-106
risk tolerance 2-72, 1-3, HDent-86
Roth IRA
   Roth IRA, filing IRS Form 8606; 5-223 and 5-242; income eligibility for contributions 5-247 and 5-249 recharacterization 5-254
   Roth IRA I-9, contributions after age 70-1/2 4-6, 5-Intro, distributions from a variable annuity 5-222
running a medical practice 2-71
Russell 1000, RMarston 28
S Curve, HDent-77, 90, 91
S&P 500 Index fund, RMarston-28; LKurtz-145
S&P 500 returns I-4, measure 2-67, associated risks 2-67, SPDRs 3-117
Salomon Brothers, RMarston-31
Sandwich generation 7-Intro
Santa Claus Effect 3-112
SBC Communications 3-118
Scott, Greg, Medsite, Intro. 10-Intro
Sears, market cap 2-63, 3-118
Self-employed Pension (SEP) 4-6, 5-Intro, non-cash contributions 5-221, contribution deadline 5-225

SEP, protected from creditors 5-230, 239; popularity 5-258
sell discipline I-7
Shering-Plough, LKurtz-142, 152, 153
Siegel, Jeremy, JSiegel-Intro
Singapore market, HDent-94, 95
Smith Barney, ABarrett-Intro
Social Security, HDent-79, 84, 88; JSiegel-38; RMarston-24
Social Security, surplus 2-58
software growth rate, ABarrett-165
SPDR 3-117
Steuger, Paul E. 3-118
stock exchanges, consolidation, RMarston-30
stock market, HDent-74, 86
stockpicker, bottom-up versus top-down, LKurtz-145
Stocks for the Long Run, JSiegel-Intro, 49
stocks
  stocks, American, RMarston-16
  stocks, consumer cyclical 3-126
  stocks, correlated with foreign stocks, RMarston-16
  stocks, European, RMarston-16
  stocks, foreign, RMarston-23; HDent-99
  stocks, high income, HDent-99
  stocks, tracking 3-128
Strategic Career management for the 21st Century Physician, GHirsch-Intro
Sun Microsystems, JSiegel-37
Supplemental Executive Retirement Plan (SERP) 4-191
systematic monthly income withdrawal 10-318
tax policy, JSiegel-40
tax shelters, HDent-86
tax, capital gains postpone paying I-12
taxes
  taxes, capital gains - mutual funds 6-258 and 6-259, rule on sale of primary residence 9-313
  taxes, estate 8-284, estate equalization 8-283, effect on IRAs 8-284
  taxes, sales, Internet, ABarrett-162, sale of overseas assets 9-310, dividends on insurance policies 9-312
  taxes, income - deduction for donating old computer 6-260, filing separately versus jointly 6-262

taxes, income, flat tax proposal 6-266, kiddie tax 6-267, interest free loans 6-269, multiple support agreement 10-320
taxes, reducing 6-Intro, dividends on insurance policies 9-312, states without income tax 6-263
taxes, multiple support agreement 10-320
tech sector trend, ABarrett-172
technology
  technology, ABarrett-Intro, 159, 163, 164, 165
  technology, broadband, ABarrett-163
  technology, gains, JSiegel-53
  technology, seasonal nature, ABarrett-160
  technology, sector, RMarston-29, LKurtz-131
telecommunication sector, LKurtz-131
Templeton, John I-2
Tenants by the Entirety 10-327
The Great Boom Ahead by Harry Dent 2-Intro
The Roaring 2000's by Harry Dent 2-Intro
third party payers, LKurtz-146; Medsite-333, 336
trade deficit, RMarston-26
trade imbalance, HDent-96, JSiegel-41
trading areas, major, HDent-97
trading halts, NYSE 3-105
trusts
  trusts, charitable remainder annuity - structure and benefits 8-287
  trusts, irrevocable life insurance (ILIT) 8-284, placing converted term policy into ILIT 9-302
  trusts, qualified marital domestic (QDOT) for non-US citizens 8-297, benefit 8-286
  trusts, qualified terminable interest property (QTIP) 10-323
  trusts, revocable living 8-284, privacy benefit 8-295
  trusts, special needs 10-321
tulip mania in Holland 2-63
unemployment, ABarrett-161, 166
Union Carbide 3-118
United Health Group (UNH), LKurtz-134
United Technologies 3-118

universities, changes over next decade, JSiegel-46
University of Pennsylvania, RMarston Intro; Medsite Intro
US economy, JSiegel-38
US Healthcare system, LKurtz-133
US Treasury market, RMarston-31
US, unemployment rate, RMarston-18
Volcker, Paul, RMarston-25
wage-price pressures, ABarrett-166
Wall Street Journal 3-118; HDent-Intro; RMarston-Intro
Wall Street Journal, comment on AMT 3-111
Wal-Mart Stores 3-118
Walt Disney 3-118
Warner Lambert, LKurtz-154
wealth effect 2-68
Weather Channel I-6
web, ABarrett-160

website
website, learn the Internet 2-73
website, Mdintellinet.com 2-74
website, Patientwatch 3-128
website, upcoming IPOs 3-125
Weiss Center for International Research, RMarston-Intro
Wharton School, University of Pennsylvania, JSiegel-Intro; RMarston Intro
wills, 8-Intro, dying without a will 8-289, selecting most favorable state 8-290, contested 10-317
Wilshire 5000 Index 3-104
Wilshire 5000 Index fund, as investment 3-109
WorldCOM (WCOM) 3-122
Worth Magazine 3-116
Xerox, RMarston-29
Y2K, remediation effort, ABarrett-163
Yen, HDent-96, 97